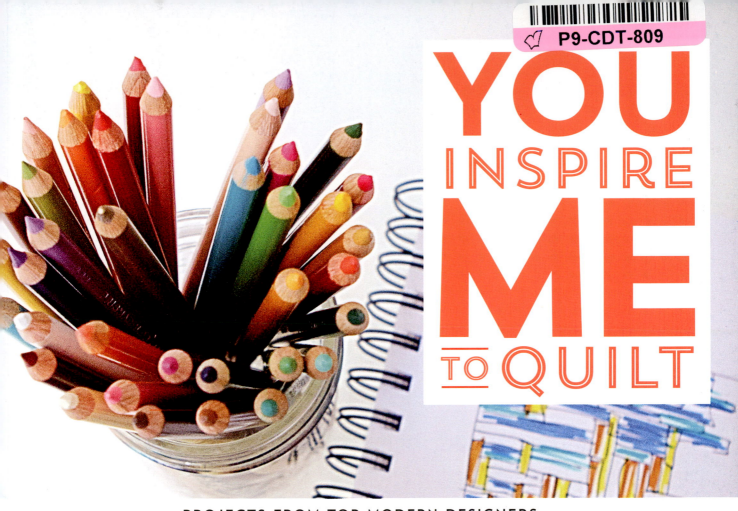

YOU INSPIRE ME TO QUILT

PROJECTS FROM TOP MODERN DESIGNERS
INSPIRED BY EVERYDAY LIFE

CHERYL ARKISON

stashBOOKS®

an imprint of C&T Publishing

Publisher | Amy Marson

Creative Director | Gailen Runge

Art Director/Book Designer |
Kristy Zacharias

Editors | Lynn Koolish and
Joanna Burgarino

Technical Editors | Helen Frost and
Nan Powell

Production Coordinators |
Freesia Pearson Blizard and Rue Flaherty

Production Editor | Katie Van Amburg

Page Layout Artist | Katie McIntosh

Illustrator | Valyrie Gillum

Photo Assistant | Mary Peyton Peppo

Style photography by Kate Inglis and
instructional photography by Diane
Pedersen, unless otherwise noted

Published by Stash Books, an imprint of C&T Publishing, Inc., P.O. Box 1456,
Lafayette, CA 94549

Library of Congress Cataloging-in-Publication Data

Arkison, Cheryl, 1975-

You inspire me to quilt : projects from top modern designers inspired by everyday life
/ Cheryl Arkison.

   pages cm

ISBN 978-1-61745-035-8 (softcover)

1. Patchwork--Patterns. 2. Quilting--Patterns. 3. Quiltmakers. I. Title.

TT835.A7424 2015

746.46--dc23

                    2014033372

Printed in China

10 9 8 7 6 5 4 3 2 1

CONTENTS

PROJECTS

DEDICATION

For Meredith Helgeson, who pushed me to become my own quilter

ACKNOWLEDGMENTS

Thank you to my husband, Morgan, for planting the earworm, for encouraging me despite his own stress, and for providing the opportunity to pursue my dreams. And to my children for continually hoping that this book will finally make me the famous quilter they so want me to be.

Thank you to Kate Inglis for letting me dump my ideas, churning them up, and then helping me pick them up off the beach. And for the collaboration when taking photos.

Thank you to Anna Grose and Jenn Jones for the continued support, babysitting, and understanding when I get a bit too crazy.

Thank you to all the contributors. And thank you to Lynn Koolish and the folks at C&T for making this a wickedly fun book to work on. It was tremendously inspiring for me.

Thank you to the companies that continue to invent and expand the portable technology that allows us quilters to capture the inspiration and sparks we see every single day.

Finally, thank you to all the quilters out there who snap photos, steal their kids' markers, jot down ideas on grocery store receipts, and daydream in the school pickup line. You are the ones who inspire me to keep creating.

INTRODUCTION

My husband is extremely supportive of my quilting, often lending an eye or an ear to design dilemmas. I have to say, though, that his obsession with me making a certain quilt got out of hand. He mentioned it at least once a month for years. He brainstormed the inspiration, drew sketches, and got giddy thinking about it. Would he pick up a rotary cutter and make it himself? Heck, no! Instead, he kept pestering me until I made the quilt.

So I did. And it inspired this book.

In telling the story to other quilters, I discovered that I wasn't the only one hounded by the ideas and concepts of the nonquilters around me. So many more husbands, friends, parents, kids, and even store clerks had these ideas of what could make a cool quilt. Not all of them are feasible for a functional quilt (*chain mail*?), but most are indeed doable. Not all of them are immediately apparent as doable, but with some pestering and festering, the concept can become reality.

These ideas become quilts because they are a challenge. Despite the frustration, the limitations of the materials, and the walls of insecurity we build, we get satisfaction from rising to the occasion. Whether it is as simple as matching points or figuring out how to translate bacon into a quilt, I think there are two reasons why we do this.

One, we enjoy the technical aspect of the challenge. We are constantly pushing ourselves, whether we know it or not. With every quilt we make, our skills grow. Each quilt is often a little more difficult than the one we just finished. So taking on the seemingly impossible task of making a map quilt inspired by fantasy role-playing games is a creative challenge that can be hard to ignore.

And two, when those requests come from people we care about, it is difficult (impossible?) to say no. Whether they nag us to the point of an earworm or merely mention the idea in passing, we can't help but want to make them happy. It's what quilters do. More often than not the quilts we make are for others; it's just that this time they are giving us the design idea instead of us trying the latest pattern. It is our loved ones providing the spark to our creativity.

It is then up to us to translate that spark of inspiration into an actual quilt. In all honesty, this is where many of us get bogged down. Just how do you take that nostalgic memory of Saturday nights watching hockey and actually turn it into a quilt? What is the process for designing, pattern drafting, and finishing the quilt?

This book captures the story of how we (myself and eight other quilters) did just that. Husbands, partners, nephews, and friends provided the spark. Sometimes working in silence, building to a surprise, and sometimes working collaboratively with our loved ones, we all took on the challenge to create these quilts. And we documented the creative process so we could share it with you.

The quilts in this book are a combination of the seemingly ridiculous and the absurdly cool. The inspirations range from technology to fantasy. The quilts are all made to function—they are intended to be wrapped around legs, used as fort walls, or cuddled with on the sofa. At the same time, these are most definitely not Grandma's bed quilts!

Each quilt we make is a story and has a story. From the simple *I just wanted to try this pattern* or *I really liked the fabric* to *I stopped on the side of the road to take a picture of a sign*. The stories are inextricably tied to the quilt.

The projects in this book are broken down into as much detail and specific instruction as possible for that specific quilt. But if you are inspired to make your own date stamp quilt, feel free to change it up and make it your own. We are all dealing with similar creative challenges, the same demands on our time, and the never-ending push and pull of translating inspiration. Not to mention the requests from our loved ones.

While an equalizer-inspired quilt may not be on your own honey-do list, you might be able to persuade your own audiophile to add it instead of the turntable idea he had—why not? The kinks are already worked out for you.

It's easy to get caught up in the inspiration and ideas found online. If the digital realm ever gets overwhelming or discouraging, don't hesitate to turn off the computer or take a break from social media. So much of what we see online is an edited or manufactured view of the world. Remember that all quilters struggle with finding the time and only share what they want to share—as opposed to all of it. Keep this in mind when something seems too good to be true.

If group therapy has taught us anything, it is that we are not alone in our struggles. In chronicling the journey of a group of quilters from the initial inspiration to the final stitches, we get ideas of how to face and surmount the obstacles that are in the way. These ideas provide not only insight into the creative process but inspiration as well.

ON SEWING

The quilts in this book range from simple to complex. The quilters who made them were focused on making the quilts they needed to make, the ones that complete their stories. They weren't focused on making a twin-size quilt, for example. So the sizes vary widely, as do the techniques. But the following basics run across all the quilts.

- All yardage requirements are based on a 40˝ width of fabric (WOF). If your fabrics are wider than 40˝ after you cut the selvages off, that's okay.

- Press, or wash and press, your fabric before you cut.

- Cut carefully. Take the time to cut all your pieces the exact size you need them to be.

- Piece accurately. Use a scant ¼˝ seam allowance unless otherwise stated.

- Backing and batting sizes are 4˝ larger than the quilt top.

- Piece your quilt backs as necessary or look for wide fabric designed specifically for backings.

- When personalizing a quilt, make sure to adjust your material requirements for backing, batting, and binding.

- Bindings are all made from 2˝- or 2½˝-wide strips, folded in half lengthwise and pressed. The raw edges are sewn to the quilt and the folded edge is brought to the back for stitching. This is called a double-fold binding.

- Start your project with a new sewing machine needle and keep your machine clean.

- Enjoy the process, from beginning to end.

There are many ways to change a pattern to suit your style, your skill level, and the recipient's taste. Add or subtract blocks. Change the size of the block. Introduce negative space to the design. Increase the proportions of the quilt. All of these suggestions can help you personalize your quilt, making it part of your story.

For a refresher or resource on basic techniques, the following books are excellent to have on the bookshelf:

The Practical Guide to Patchwork, by Elizabeth Hartman (from Stash Books)

Sunday Morning Quilts, by Amanda Jean Nyberg and Cheryl Arkison (from Stash Books)

Quilting Modern, by Jacquie Gering and Katie Pedersen (from Interweave)

QuiltEssential, by Erin Burke Harris (from Stash Books)

FROM THE FIRST DANCE

INSPIRATION

" My husband, Morgan, is a guy who listens to music a lot and likes it loud with a lot of bass. Back when stereos were assembled with components housed in black boxes—one for the tapes, one for the radio, one for the record player, and eventually one for the CDs—a true audiophile had an equalizer to make it all sound better. A side benefit of many equalizers was the dancing lights they produced in time with the music. And according to Morgan, another benefit was providing the perfect quilt inspiration.

It was actually a lot of fun collaborating with Morgan on this quilt. He has a great eye for design (well, for knowing what is good). I actually wish he would get involved in the quilting a bit more because he has some excellent ideas.

You Inspire Me to Quilt

PROCESS

We went back and forth on the final design of this quilt. The question was whether Morgan wanted it to look like a piece of furniture or a piece of stereo equipment. I also wanted to know if he wanted a literal interpretation or if I could be a bit more liberal with the inspiration. In the end, we agreed that the inspiration of the dancing colors was the most important aspect to capture.

While I generally work improvisationally, I had to put aside those instincts and plan out this quilt in detail. We had to capture the right image and draft the pattern to go with it. It was a challenge, but a rather fun one.

CHERYL…ON INSPIRATION

One of my favorite things about my sketchbooks is that they serve as a sort of journal record of my life, not just quilt ideas. I date my sketches and often include a little note about the inspiration—what struck me in particular, what I was feeling, or where exactly I was when the inspiration hit. I'm not actually that great at drawing, so the note helps me.

And with my kids getting older, they contribute to the sketchbook too—whether with a specific quilt idea or just something random jotted down while waiting for dinner in a restaurant. I think I would rescue my sketchbooks from a fire before I would rescue my quilts. They are too tied to me and my history to lose.

Photos by Cheryl Arkison

CHERYL ARKISON

EQUALIZER

FINISHED BLOCK: 4″ × 3″

FINISHED QUILT: 88″ × 71″

Materials Required

- **Medium green:** ⅓ yard for bar blocks
- **Light green:** ⅓ yard for bar blocks
- **Lemon yellow:** ⅓ yard for bar blocks
- **Golden yellow:** ⅓ yard for bar blocks
- **Orange:** ¼ yard for bar blocks
- **Red:** ¼ yard for bar blocks
- **Black:** 5 yards for background, sashing, and borders
- **Backing fabric:** 5¼ yards (pieced crosswise)
- **Binding fabric:** ¾ yard
- **Batting:** 92˝ × 75˝

Cutting Instructions

WOF = width of fabric

COLORED FABRIC:

- Cut the colored fabrics in 2½˝ × WOF strips.

    Dark green: 3 strips

    Light green: 3 strips

    Lemon yellow: 3 strips

    Golden yellow: 3 strips

    Orange: 2 strips

    Red: 2 strips

BLACK:

Bars and column sashing:

- Cut 31 strips 1½˝ × WOF.
- Cut 2 strips 2½˝ × WOF; subcut into 13 rectangles 2½˝ × 4½˝.

Bar ends:

- Cut 6 strips 4½˝ × WOF; subcut into the following:

    2 strips 4½˝ × 30½˝

    2 strips 4½˝ × 24½˝

    3 strips 4½˝ × 18½˝

    3 strips 4½˝ × 12½˝

    3 strips 4½˝ × 6½˝

Borders:

- Cut 7 strips 12½˝ × WOF.

Binding:

- Cut 9 strips 2½˝ × WOF.

ASSEMBLY

Make the Bar Blocks

1. Sew each colored strip to a 1½˝ black strip. Press the seam open or toward the colored strip.

> **TIP**
>
> *This is the time to press, not iron, your strips. Do not push the iron along the fabric. Rather, place the iron on the seam and then raise and lower it as you move down the seam. This will keep the long strip sets from stretching and distorting.*

2. Cut the strip sets from Step 1 into 4½˝ sections to make the bar blocks.

Medium green: Cut 26.

Light green: Cut 26.

Lemon yellow: Cut 24.

Golden yellow: Cut 20.

Orange: Cut 15.

Red: Cut 12.

Cut sections to make bar blocks.

Assemble the Quilt Top

1. Sew the bar blocks, black bars, and bar ends together according to the column assembly chart (below) and the quilt assembly diagram (page 17). Press all the seams open or toward the colored pieces. Be careful not to stretch the columns.

Column Assembly

Column A (Make 2.)	Column B (Make 3.)	Column C (Make 3.)	Column D (Make 2.)	Column E (Make 3.)
2 dark green	2 dark green	2 dark green	2 dark green	2 dark green
2 light green	2 light green	2 light green	2 light green	2 light green
1 black bar	2 lemon yellow	2 lemon yellow	2 lemon yellow	2 lemon yellow
1 lemon yellow	2 golden yellow	2 golden yellow	1 black bar	2 golden yellow
30½˝ bar end	1 black bar	2 orange	1 golden yellow	2 orange
	1 orange	2 red	24½˝ bar end	1 black bar
	18½˝ bar end	1 black bar		1 red
		1 red		12½˝ bar end
		6½˝ bar end		

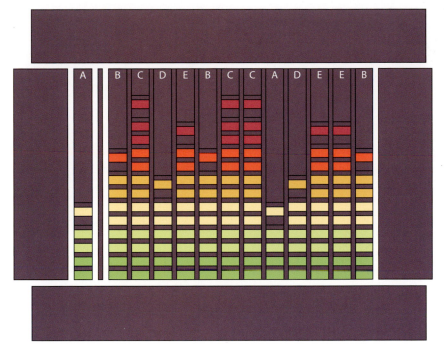

Quilt assembly

TIP

Label each column as you complete it. Pin a scrap of paper or place a piece of tape marked with the column name on the bottom piece. That way you won't have to remove it when you add the bar end pieces.

2. Lay out the columns according to the quilt assembly diagram (above) or rearrange them to suit your own preference.

3. Sew the 15 remaining black 1½″ × WOF strips together end to end. Cut 12 pieces 1½″ × 47½″ for the column sashing.

NOTE

Depending on the width of the black fabric you are using, you may need only 14, not 15, strips.

4. To prevent stretching, pin the columns to the sashing pieces (all but the far left column). Sew and press toward the column, not the sashing. Join together all the columns and sashing in this fashion.

5. Sew 7 strips 12½″ × WOF of border fabric together end to end. Cut 2 pieces 12½″ × 47½″ and 2 pieces 12½″ × 88½″.

6. Pin and sew the 12½″ × 47½″ pieces to the sides. Press toward the columns.

7. Pin and sew the 12½″ × 88½″ pieces to the top and bottom. Press toward the columns.

TIP

To minimize or prevent distortion on all these long seams, alternate sewing from top to bottom and from bottom to top as you sew the columns together.

Finish the Quilt

1. Make the quilt backing. Go for something fun, maybe with a nod to the stereo equipment. Perhaps some circuitry or wood grain? Or, pull from the colors of the quilt top.

2. Create a quilt sandwich by layering the pieced top, batting, and backing. Secure the sandwich together using your preferred method of basting to prevent the layers from shifting while you are quilting.

3. For quilting, it would be time-consuming but not difficult to outline each colored bar. An allover pattern also works well. Try variegated or black thread. Or you can do as I did and extend the concept of sound into the quilting. I chose to echo curves, like a sound wave, emanating from a corner.

CHERYL…ON FLOW

I usually have multiple projects ongoing in various states of readiness and doneness. That means I can work on the appropriate project for the head space I'm in. For example, I can't do precision piecing when I'm feeling antsy. I need improv to calm me down. Or if I'm making a quilt for someone specific I have to be thinking good things about the person to tackle that project. Because of this I do not feel all that anxious about the number of works in progress hiding in my closets.

BINDING

Square up the quilt. Make and apply the binding; finish by hand or machine. A black binding will not take away from the dancing lights. This quilt could also be faced instead of bound.

CHERYL...ON TEACHING

Quite often, I teach for guilds, where the students know each other well. They invite me into their lives as they catch up and gossip as much as they sew. So many students come to a class not just to learn something, but to get a day or evening off from their real lives. It is a treat that they choose to share that precious time with me.

BACON MAKES EVERYTHING BETTER

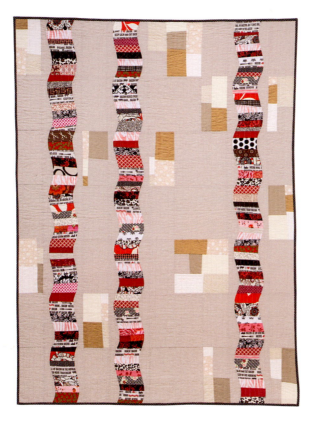

INSPIRATION

"Cynthia's immediate family is Norm and two sweet dog "fur babies," Starr and Charlie. Norm provided the inspiration for this quilt. It was all about the bacon.

Cynthia took this inspiration almost literally, but she translated the design with fabric, not in the kitchen. She started by designing the wavy bacon templates to make them the focus. She even went so far to as to design some bacon-inspired fabric to use in the quilt—you can get some for yourself from Spoonflower (spoonflower.com > search "i heart bacon!").

PROCESS

Because they work together in their daily life, it isn't surprising that Cynthia often turns to Norm when working on a quilt. She shows him parts as she goes, and Norm acts as a consultant or art director. And he helps on the part of the quiltmaking process that Cynthia likes the least—making the quilt sandwich.

CYNTHIA…ON INSPIRATION

People who get stuff done inspire me—especially those who are professional and respectful to others during the process. People who are out doing their thing, being who they are, creating and making and doing, not worrying about what others think of them and not being afraid to just go for it and get what they want and make their mark, whatever way they want to do it. No excuses, no fear, just getting it done. That's important and inspiring to me.

Photos by Cynthia Frenette

CYNTHIA FRENETTE

FUNKY BACON!

FINISHED BLOCKS: 7⅜″ × 9½″ | 4½″ × 9½″ | 9½″ × 9½″

FINISHED QUILT: 49⅝″ × 66½″

Materials Required

- **Assorted print scraps:** 2 yards total for wave blocks
- **Light fabric:** 3 yards for main background
- **Assorted light fabrics:** 6 fat quarters in similar tones as main background fabric

TIP

You can use assorted fabrics that are similar in color to the main background fabric but different enough to be noticeable, or you can go wild and crazy and make them all very different! Make your quilt however you like.

- **Backing fabric:** 2⅛ yards at least 42″ wide (plus quilt top leftovers)
- **Binding fabric:** ⅝ yard
- **Batting:** 54″ × 71″

CYNTHIA...ON MAKING MISTAKES

Own your work! Don't apologize or make excuses for any technical error or oversight, which I call "happy accidents." You just made a beautiful quilt!

NOTE

You will need 2 background pieces per block. Each pattern piece (page 31) is the same size and shape for the sides of each block. Enlarge, then trace or copy the background pattern.

__If you are using a solid fabric for your background and the right side doesn't matter,__ use the background pattern to cut 42 pieces.

__If you are using a print or a fabric with a definite right side,__ fold your fabric in half so it is wrong sides together and cut 2 pieces at a time. You'll end up with 2 pieces, 1 and 1 reversed, for the backgrounds of each block (for a total of 21 pairs, or 42 pieces altogether).

Cutting Instructions

WOF = width of fabric

ASSORTED PRINT SCRAPS:

- Cut strips, each 1″–3″ wide × 6″.

LIGHT FABRIC:

- Cut 42 block backgrounds (page 31).

NOTE

These amounts include enough for a pieced backing, the instructions for which are included.

- Cut 1 square 12″ × 12″.
- Cut 15 squares 10″ × 10″.

    Subcut 10 squares in half, into 5″ × 10″ pieces, for 20 total.

ASSORTED LIGHT FABRICS:

- Cut 1 square 12″ × 12″ from each fat quarter, for 6 total.
- Cut 1 rectangle 5″ × 10″ from each fat quarter, for 6 total.

BINDING FABRIC:

- Cut 7 strips 2¼″ × WOF.

ASSEMBLY

Make the Scrappy Wave Blocks

1. Enlarge, then trace or copy 21 wave patterns (page 31). You will need 1 paper wave pattern per block to use for paper piecing.

2. Cut out around the outer lines of the paper wave pattern.

> **TIP**
>
> *You can use foundation piecing instead of paper piecing if you prefer. Trace the pattern onto a muslin foundation instead of using paper. Don't forget to transfer the pivot marks to the foundation.*

3. Place the paper wave pattern right side up. Place a print strip on top, right side up, so that the raw edges hang over the edges of the paper and slightly over the far left edge. Be sure to have some overage, as you will trim the piece after covering the entire piece with fabric strips.

4. Place another strip of fabric right sides together with the first piece, aligning the raw edges on the right and ensuring that you have sufficient fabric beyond the edges of the paper.

5. Shorten your stitch length. Sew the pieces together, sewing through the paper and using a ¼˝ seam allowance. Flip open the fabric piece you just sewed. Press, but do not use steam as this distorts the fabric.

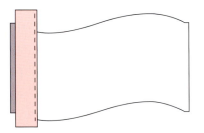

Adding strips of fabric

6. Repeat Steps 4 and 5 until the pattern piece is entirely covered in fabric strips.

> **TIP**
>
> *Piece together shorter pieces of different fabrics to make strips if you want an extra-scrappy look.*

7. Flip the piece over so the foundation is on top. Using a rotary cutter, carefully trim away the excess fabric from the outer edges of the foundation, leaving a ¼˝ seam allowance. Scissors are helpful when cutting around the end tabs.

8. Transfer the pivot pattern markings to the wrong side of the fabric. Transfer the marks indicated on the curved edges of the wave piece to the right side of your fabric, keeping the marks small and within the ¼˝ seam allowance area.

> **TIP**
>
> *It is absolutely essential to the accuracy of the block to transfer the marks as indicated. The marks ensure that the blocks join correctly into a continuous wave when they are all sewn together. Take the time to mark the pieces and your blocks will align easily and come out beautifully!*

9. Remove the paper backing and set the wave piece aside.

10. Repeat Steps 1–9 to make 21 wave pieces. Set aside.

Add the Background

1. Transfer the pivot marks to the wrong side of the fabric on all the wave background pieces. Transfer the marks indicated on the curved edges of the piece to the right side of your fabric, keeping the marks small and within the ¼˝ seam allowance area.

2. Place a background piece on top of a wave piece, right sides together. Line up the ends and the pivot marks. Pin them together. It is important to *pin the ends in place first* to hold the background pieces accurately in place and to keep the fabric and overall block from distorting as you sew the curved seams. Next pin the pieces together, matching each mark that you made along the curved edges. The pieces will buckle, but as long as the marks are matching this is fine.

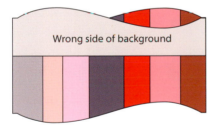

Lining up wave and background pieces

3. Sew the first seam using a ¼˝ seam allowance. Keeping the background piece on the top and the wave piece on the bottom, start at a raw edge and sew straight across to the first pivot mark. Stop at the mark with your needle down and lift the presser foot. Slightly lift the edge of the background fabric under the presser foot and then reach under and gently tug the wave piece's raw edge to align with the background piece's raw edge. The fabric will flatten out and form the curved edge once aligned.

Once you have the raw edges aligned, pivot the piece, lower the presser foot, and continue sewing with a ¼˝ seam allowance. Align the raw edges as you go and turn the pieces to follow the curved edge.

> **TIP**
>
> *Do not stretch the fabric to fit or try to straighten the seam; it will align and flatten out as you sew. Let your machine do the work to aid in sewing a nice flat, curved seam.*

4. Continue sewing until you reach the last pivot mark. Stop at the mark, put the needle down, pivot the entire piece so that you keep a ¼˝ seam allowance, lower the presser foot, and sew to the raw edge. Remove the last pins.

5. Using sharp scissors, snip close to the pivot marks but not through the stitching. This will allow the curved seam allowance to lie flat. Flip the pieces open and you will notice that the seam allowance will want to fall naturally to one side. Lightly finger-press into place; then press with an iron without using steam.

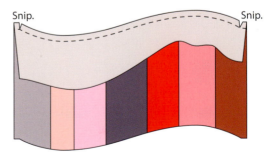

Snip seam allowance.

6. Repeat Steps 2–5 to add the other background piece to the wave piece.

7. Repeat to make 21 blocks.

Join the Blocks into Columns

1. Arrange 3 columns of 7 blocks each.

2. Place 2 blocks right sides together so that the wave seams, pivot marks, and raw edges match.

> **TIP**
>
> *To help precisely align the blocks so that the curved seams match up, take a pin and insert it through a pivot mark, going from the back of the top block through the front of the bottom block so the marks align, and then pin in place. Repeat with the second pivot mark, pinning the pieces together.*

3. Sew the 2 blocks together using a precise ¼˝ seam allowance, making sure to sew through each pivot mark. Press the seam open.

4. Continue joining blocks to make 3 columns. Set aside.

Assemble the Background Blocks

1. Place 7 squares 12˝ × 12˝ (1 main background fabric square and 6 different fat quarter squares) in a pile on the cutting mat with the raw edges aligned and the right sides up.

2. Using a rotary cutter and a ruler, cut the stack into 7 pieces through all the layers of fabric. You can cut them into any arrangement, and as wonky as you like, as long as there are 7 pieces total when you're done.

Stack and cut.

3. Shuffle the pieces as follows so each block will have 1 piece of each fabric in it once it's sewn:

From pile 1, take the top piece and move it to the bottom of its pile.

From pile 2, take the top 2 pieces and move them to the bottom of their pile.

From pile 3, take the top 3 pieces and move them to the bottom of their pile.

From pile 4, take the top 4 pieces and move them to the bottom of their pile.

From pile 5, take the top 5 pieces and move them to the bottom of their pile.

From pile 6, take the top 6 pieces and move them to the bottom of their pile.

Leave pile 7 as is and do not shuffle.

4. Using only the top-layer pieces from each pile, sew pieces 1 and 2 with right sides together. Press. Set aside.

TIP

Lay the just-sewn pieces on top of the pile to keep track of the order.

5. Sew pieces 3, 4, and 5 with right sides together. Then sew pieces 6 and 7 with right sides together. Press after each seam.

6. Place your first row (pieces 1 and 2) right sides together with the second row (pieces 3, 4, and 5), aligning the raw edges. The rows will not be equal lengths anymore. You will trim all the blocks later. Align the 2 rows and sew together. Repeat with row 3, attaching it to the bottom of row 2. Press all the seams to one side.

7. Repeat Steps 4–6 for all the remaining pieces to make a total of 7 finished blocks.

8. Trim each block to 10˝ × 10˝. If you wish, slightly turn each block before you cut it for an extra wonky look.

9. Once you have trimmed all 7 blocks, set 2 aside. Take the remaining 5 blocks and cut each in half, so that you end up with 10 pieced rectangles 5˝ × 10˝. Set these aside.

Assemble the Quilt Top

1. Following the quilt assembly diagram (at right), arrange the 3 columns of wave blocks and the background pieces into columns as shown. When you're happy with the layout, begin assembling the background blocks into columns, sewing each piece to the next using a ¼˝ seam allowance, right sides together. Press the seams open.

NOTE

Column 5 is a bit different: the pieces are first assembled in pairs horizontally and then joined into a column.

2. Join the columns using a ¼˝ seam allowance, with right sides together. Press the seams open.

Quilt assembly

Assemble the Quilt Back

1. Use the remaining assorted fabric strips to make a piece 6″ × 72″ and trim it to 5½″ × 72″. Set aside.

2. Make another piece, starting and ending with the remaining 5″ × 10″ main background fabric pieces so that each end of the strip is the same fabric. Arrange the remaining 5″ × 10″ fat quarter pieces, in no particular order, in between the ends. Sew the pieces together to make a piece measuring 5″ × 76½″. Trim 2¼″ off each end to make the piece 72″ long.

3. Measure the backing fabric. If your fabric isn't 42″ wide, add a strip of coordinating fabric. Trim the backing to 42″ × 72″. Sew the 5½″ × 72″ piece from Step 1 to the left edge of the 42″ × 72″ piece of backing fabric with a ¼″ seam. Press the seam to one side.

4. Sew the 5″ × 72″ piece from Step 2 to the right edge of the 42″ × 72″ piece of backing fabric with a ¼″ seam. Press the seam to one side.

5. Fold the backing piece in half lengthwise and sew the pieced edges together with a ¼″ seam to form a tube. Smooth the entire piece and press the fold. Using scissors, cut on the fold. Open the piece. The scrappy pieces will be down the middle of the backing.

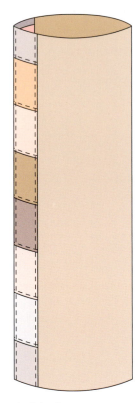

Quilt back piecing

6. Open and press the seams again and the back is done!

Finish the Quilt

1. Create a quilt sandwich by layering the pieced top, batting, and backing. Secure the sandwich together using your preferred method of basting to prevent shifting while you are quilting.

2. Quilt as desired. Cynthia quilted her quilt using wonky vertical lines with varying space between them—no measuring or precision, just grab your walking foot and go! Feel free to quilt your waves and your background with different motifs as well to emphasize the bacon design.

BINDING

Square up the quilt. Make and apply the binding; finish by hand or machine.

Admire your wild and crazy bacony waves. As Norm says, "Everything is better with bacon on it!"

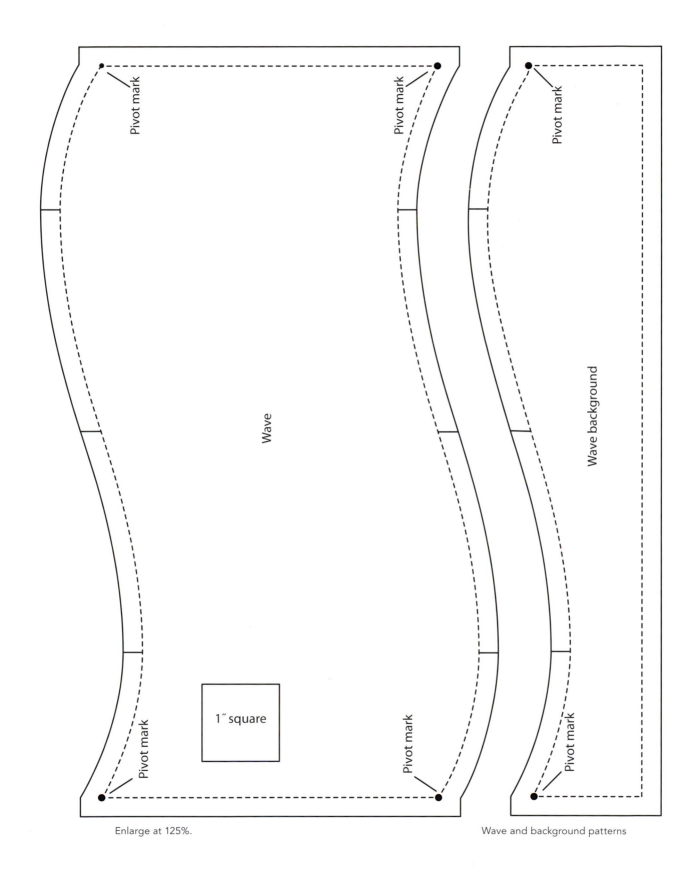

Pivot mark

Pivot mark

Pivot mark

Wave

Pivot mark

Pivot mark

Pivot mark

Wave background

Pivot mark

Pivot mark

1″ square

Enlarge at 125%.

Wave and background patterns

QUILTMAKER
Cynthia Frenette

Photo by Cynthia Frenette

Fabric has always been the base of Cynthia's work, starting with the first dress and quilts she ever made. Now she has her own fabric lines with Robert Kaufman.

As a graphic designer and illustrator, Cynthia works happily with a pen and paper and on the computer. This helps her as a quilter, too. She can start with an idea or a sketch and then hit the computer to make an actual pattern.

Cynthia works directly with her husband, Norm, in their design business. It was he who inspired this quilt, or perhaps he just played the bacon card to get what he wanted. Says Norm, "I'm a bit of a quilt widower! It gives me lots of time to play video games and eat bacon as well as think up recipes that I can add bacon to."

Visit Cynthia's website at cynthiaf.ca.

CYNTHIA…ON IMPROV

Improv to me is working freely with colors and shapes and making art with fabric. It's my favorite way of working. I love the freedom to go with what I feel rather than following a set pattern, layout, or style. If something doesn't work, take it out or change it. If something is really working, build on it. Make it work and go with what feels right!

CYNTHIA…ON TAKING OFF

Don't be afraid to just go for it. You can't ruin anything and you learn a lot with every quilt you make. Trust your instincts.

“ I usually help sandwich quilts, and everyone knows that bacon goes good with a sandwich.

—*Norm (Cynthia's husband)*

INSPIRING EACH OTHER

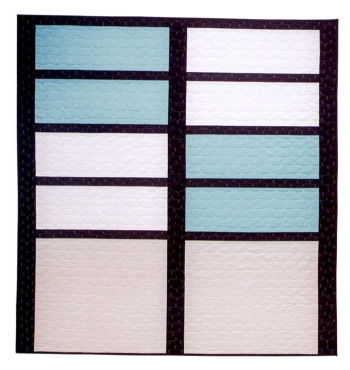

INSPIRATION

" The inspiration for this quilt hit both Heather and her husband, Jeff, together. It might have been kismet. They were leaving an exhibit and saw a sign in a parking lot. Both of them were drawn to the graphic qualities of the structure and the symmetrical use of bright colors, especially in an item that most people would probably never see or pay any attention to. After photographing the sign, Heather pulled out her sketchbook, as she always does.

With two artists in the house, it is easy to see how they inspire each other: Heather made the quilt and Jeff has since said he would like to make a painting of the same inspiration, although he normally works on a much smaller scale.

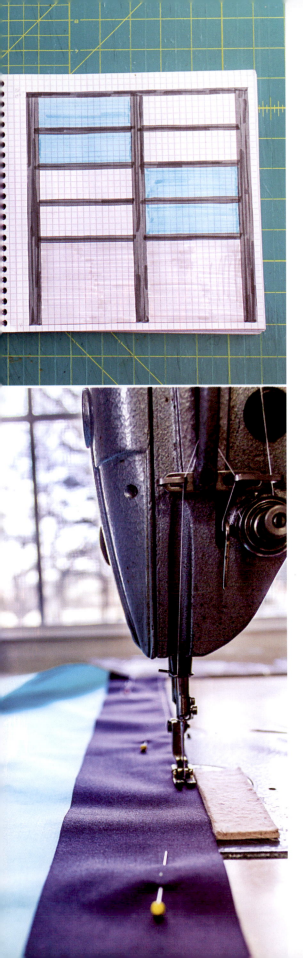

PROCESS

Heather works in solids most often, so part of her process is determining the right combination of fabrics. With so many solid fabrics available, this is both a challenging and an exciting part of the process.

Note: Heather included the specific fabrics if you want to replicate the quilt exactly. Of course, you should feel perfectly free to use any color or fabric you like. Kona cottons are a full 44˝ wide; if you use narrower fabrics, purchase 1⅓ yards each of the blue and white and cut the pieces widthwise, not lengthwise.

HEATHER … ON DESIGN

From the start, I have always designed my own quilts. Designing quilts and patterns is actually my favorite part of the process, so it's much more exciting to me to do that rather than create something from another pattern. That being said, one day I will make Denyse Schmidt's *Single Girl* quilt!

Photos by Heather Jones

HEATHER JONES

SIGN

FINISHED QUILT: 72˝ × 76˝

Materials Required

- **Blue (Kona Azure):** 1 yard
- **White (Kona White):** 1 yard
- **Light gray (Kona Silver):** 1¾ yards
- **Dark gray (Kona Charcoal):** 2¼ yards for sashing and borders
- **Backing fabric (Kona Silver):** 4⅝ yards
- **Binding fabric (Kona Charcoal):** ⅔ yard
- **Batting:** 76″ × 80″

Cutting Instructions

WOF = width of fabric

BLUE:

- Cut 1 strip 30½″ × WOF.

  Subcut the strip *lengthwise* into 4 pieces 30½″ × 10½″.

WHITE:

- Cut 1 strip 30½″ × WOF.

  Subcut the strip *lengthwise* into 4 pieces 30½″ × 10½″.

LIGHT GRAY:

- Cut 2 strips 26½″ × WOF.

  Trim each strip so that it measures 26½″ × 30½″.

DARK GRAY:

- Cut 1 strip 74½″ × WOF.

  Subcut the strip *lengthwise* into 3 pieces 4½″ × 74½″ for vertical sashing and side borders.

  Subcut the strip *lengthwise* into 5 pieces 2½″ × 74½″. Subcut each of 4 pieces into 2 pieces 2½″ × 30½″ for a total of 8 pieces for horizontal sashing.

  Trim the remaining piece to 2½″ × 72½″ for the top border.

BINDING:

- Cut 8 strips 2½″ × WOF.

ASSEMBLY

Assemble the Quilt Top

Quilt assembly

1. Following the quilt assembly diagram (above), arrange and sew the pieces into 2 columns, each with 2 pieces of blue and white, 1 piece of light gray, and 4 horizontal sashing pieces of dark gray. Press the seams toward the sashing fabric.

2. Sew the pieced columns to the vertical sashing piece. Press the seams toward the sashing fabric.

3. Add the side border pieces. Press the seams toward the borders.

4. Add the top border piece. Press the seams toward the border.

Finish the Quilt

1. Make the quilt backing.

2. Create a quilt sandwich by layering the pieced top, batting, and backing. Secure the sandwich together using your preferred method of basting to prevent shifting while you are quilting.

3. Quilt as desired. Heather uses a signature wishbone quilting design on most of her quilts. Be inspired to create your own style, or choose something to take advantage of the negative space in this design.

> **TIP**
>
> *Use quilting gloves (which can be as simple and inexpensive as garden gloves with silicone palms) when sewing long seams as well as when quilting. They allow your hands to have a better grip on the fabric so it can move through the sewing machine easier.*

BINDING

Square up the quilt. Make and apply the binding; finish by hand or machine.

Heather chose to bind the quilt in the same fabric as the sashing and borders. This makes the design seamless all the way to the edge.

HEATHER...ON FLOW

I always have my phone with me and use its camera function to document and capture inspiration. When I want to develop a design based on that inspiration, I hash out everything with a pencil in a sketchbook, usually a gridded one. Once everything is finalized in terms of the design, I add in color with India ink markers.

I work solely with paper, pencils, markers, and a ruler. I calculate the math for pattern pieces and yardage requirements with a calculator, but that's about all the technology that goes into my designs.

QUILTMAKER
Heather Jones

Photo by Heather Jones

When you are married to an artist and take inspiration from oft-overlooked industrial objects and buildings, it is easy to say your life is filled with creativity and beauty. When you are a busy mother to elementary school–aged kids, it is also easy to say that you have to work hard to find the space and time to create.

Heather has a quiet soul with a passion for translating her inspiration into art. She is known for graphic layouts and strong lines. Her deep love for antique quilts influences her as much as architecture and industrial objects. Her work resonates with both modern and traditional quilters.

With two active studios in the house, and two even more active children, Heather and her husband, Jeff, have carved out a life filled with creative energy. One makes large-scale graphic quilts and the other makes small, minimalist paintings, but both are inspired by seemingly uninspiring images around them.

Visit Heather's website at heatherjonesstudio.com.

HEATHER... ON FAMILY

Since quilting is more than a hobby to me, and I work out of my home studio, it's definitely a part of my day-to-day life in our house. My studio is open to my children, and I actually encourage them to come in and create with me. I try to do most of my work early in the morning before they wake up or while they are in school.

" Heather's design process and decision making influence how I approach my own art making. I look at the speed at which she works, and how places and things she sees are translated into her final designs. The scale of her work impacts me, and I often say that I wish I could make paintings as large as some of her quilts.

—Jeff (Heather's husband)

GENERATIONS OF LOVE

INSPIRATION

To the Moon was a special request from a friend of Jen's. Eréne Lejeune wanted a quilt made for her daughter, one that would go with her all the way from toddlerhood to college. As a Chinese astrologer, Eréne has a deep appreciation for the fact that she, her husband, and her daughter Vale are all born under the Virgo sign. Not to mention the magical memories of a trip to Japan and the chance find of some vintage indigo kimono scraps. Those scraps turned into a quilt Eréne had made for her husband. Now she asked Jen for a quilt incorporating the constellation Virgo and the moon phases that would also have the muted indigo tones reminiscent of the Asian aesthetic.

Creating for others is a special privilege for all creative people. It means that much more when it is for someone you know and care about.

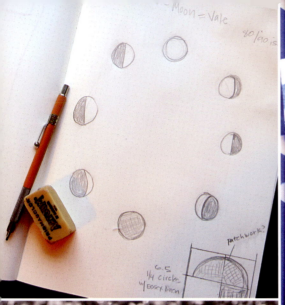

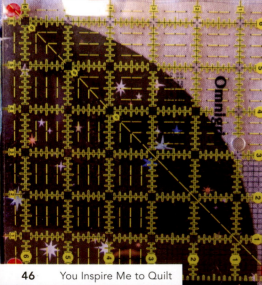

> " Whenever someone has an idea that I know I can do and I love as well, it really inspires me. It also drives me to create something that I know will be loved and cherished. I feel like the quilt is a really good representation of who Eréne is, who Vale is, and what was asked for. Any time I don't want to pass on the quilt to someone because I love it so much, that's always a good sign.

—*Jen (the designer)*

PROCESS

Jen had to research exactly what the cycles of the moon were and what Virgo looked like. A series of texts and sketches later, she settled on the final design. That same thing happened when it came time to quilting. Jen and Eréne worked with Krista Withers on the quilting design. With so much negative space, the quilting design was just as integral to the quilt as the piecing. Knowing that it was such a meaningful design for Eréne helped Jen keep her head every step of the way.

JEN…ON FLOW

When I'm making a quilt for someone, I have a ritual. I pick music that they like or that I think they'd like and listen to it from the start of the quilt to the end of the quilt.

Photos by Jen Carlton-Bailly
Quilt back photo by Diane Pedersen

JEN CARLTON-BAILLY

Quilted by Krista Withers

TO THE MOON

FINISHED BLOCK: 6˝ × 6˝

FINISHED QUILT: 80˝ × 88˝

Materials Required

- **Dark gray:** 5½ yards for background (Avoid directional prints.)

- **Assorted prints in grays, whites, and blues:** 20 scraps at least 7˝ × 7˝ for quarter moon blocks

- **Backing fabric:** 7¼ yards (pieced crosswise)

- **Binding fabric:** ¾ yard

- **Batting:** 84˝ × 92˝

- **Translucent template plastic** (*optional*)

- **Rotary cutter, 28mm** (*optional*)

Cutting Instructions

WOF = width of fabric

DARK GRAY:

- Cut 6 strips 12½˝ × WOF; subcut:

  2 pieces 16½˝ × 12½˝

  4 pieces 12½˝ × 12½˝

  4 pieces 10½˝ × 12½˝

  2 pieces 8½˝ × 12½˝

  2 pieces 6½˝ × 12½˝

  Use the leftover pieces to make 1 piece 12½˝ × 48½˝.

- Cut 4 pieces at 34½˝ × 20½˝.

- Cut 4 pieces at 34½˝ × 6½˝.

- Cut 32 concave pieces using the pattern (page 53).

- Cut 12 convex pieces using the pattern (page 53).

ASSORTED PRINTS:

- Cut 20 convex pieces using the pattern (page 53).

BINDING:

- Cut 9 strips 2¼˝ × WOF.

JEN…ON FAMILY

Finding the space for my quilting is not a problem. I'm very lucky to have a dedicated room with a door. If I need to leave a mess and walk away, I can. The time aspect is a little harder. Working full time and being a wife and a mother can make finding the time challenging. I feel grateful that I have a husband who fully supports my creative efforts. We've worked it out to make sure we both get dedicated creative—or, in his case, motorcycle/Vespa/van-building—time.

ASSEMBLY

Make the Blocks

1. Pin the concave background pieces to the convex background and moon pieces. Align the centers of the pieces and pin. Pin the ends of the pieces, ensuring that the straight edges match. Use 1 or 2 pins (more if you feel you need them) between the ends and the center pins.

TIP

To find the center, fold the pieces in half and lightly finger-press.

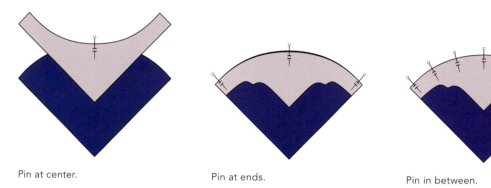

Pin at center.   Pin at ends.   Pin in between.

2. With the concave background pieces on top, sew using a scant ¼˝ seam. Go slowly until you get the hang of it. Press the seams toward the convex piece. Use a bit of spray starch or fabric stabilizer, if necessary, to help the curve lie flat. Be careful to press (lifting the iron) and not stretch the block.

NOTE

Everyone sews curves differently—using pins, no pins, or a special foot. Personally, I use pins. I find it's the best way for me to get a perfect arch.

TIP

Batching tasks helps establish a more efficient sewing routine. This simply means to pin all the pieces, sew them all, press them all, and finally square them all up. One task at a time.

3. Make 32 blocks.

4. Square up the blocks to 6½˝ × 6½˝.

TIP

Use a 6½˝ × 6½˝ square ruler along with a rotating self-healing cutting mat to square the blocks quickly and accurately.

5. Assemble and sew together the quarter-circle blocks in groups of 4, according to the quilt assembly diagram (page 51).

Assemble the Quilt Top

1. Arrange and sew the blocks to the background pieces as shown in the quilt assembly diagram (below). Press toward the background pieces.

2. Assemble the pieces into 3 columns. Join the columns, taking care to match the seams. Press toward the background pieces.

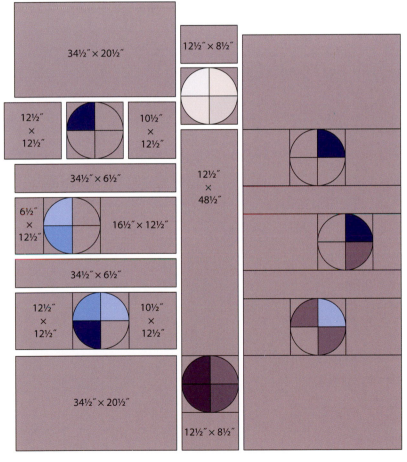

Quilt assembly

JEN … ON MAKING MISTAKES

When quilters ask for advice, I say, "Don't try so hard to be perfect; instead learn the process. You can perfect it later."

Finish the Quilt

1. Make the quilt backing. Jen made her backing a representation of the Virgo constellation.

2. Create a quilt sandwich by layering the pieced top, batting, and backing. Secure the sandwich together using your preferred method of basting to prevent shifting while you are quilting.

3. Quilt as desired. This quilt was quilted by longarmer Krista Withers. During the consultation, Krista, Jen, and Eréne chose a design that would echo the astrology and phases of the moon theme. With the abundance of negative space, the pattern provides ample opportunity to bring movement and additional detail to the quilt.

BINDING

Square up the quilt. Make and apply the binding; finish by hand or machine.

Jen is a quilter who enjoys binding. She finds it a treat to slow down and hand stitch. On a meaningful quilt such as this, it is a moment to reflect on the process and the recipient. While binding she will say her recipient's name over and over in her head because she truly puts so much of herself spiritually into her quilts.

JEN…ON IMPROV

When I first experimented with improv I didn't get it. It made me uncomfortable and anxious. Now, it's something that I love to do. Improv to me means letting the fabric decide the shape and pattern. I find that using scraps is best for me, beginning with a favorite piece and building from there.

Convex and concave patterns

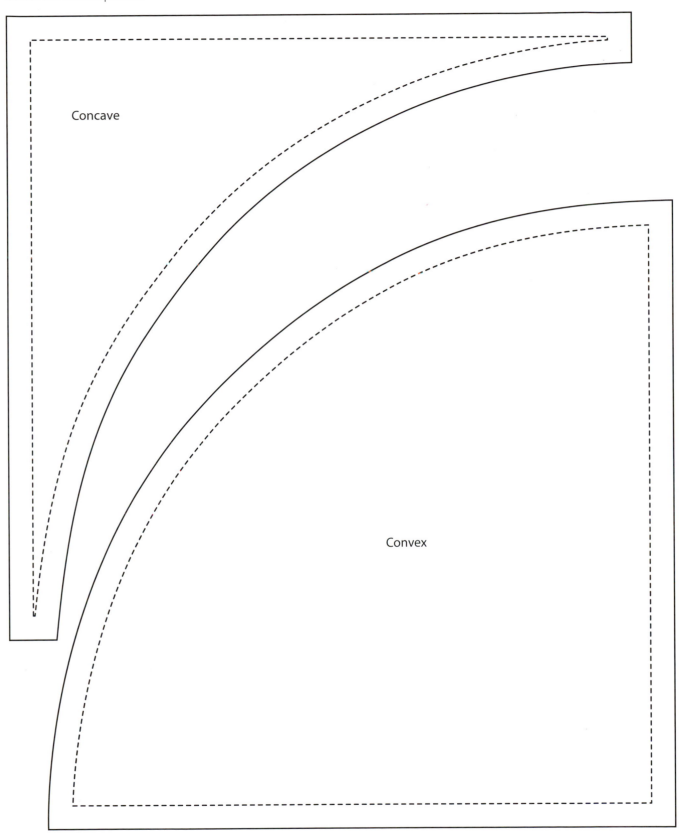

Concave

Convex

QUILTMAKER
Jen Carlton-Bailly

Photo by Jen Carlton-Bailly

Even in the midst of chaos and stress you will always find a smile on Jen Carlton-Bailly's face. She surrounds herself with the energy of her kids, her husband, and her friends and the creativity of the Modern Quilt Guild. When you've been quilting for more than 15 years, it is easy to embrace the beauty all around. Living in Portland, Oregon, and playing around with vintage Vespa scooters helps too.

Jen's first quilt was made after her daughter was born prematurely. During her time in the NICU she was given a quilt. Years later, her daughter still carries that quilt. After seeing the love and support that could come from a quilt, Jen was inspired to learn how to quilt in order to give back.

Jen is a quilter who knows what she likes yet keeps herself open to inspiration. Whether it is from friends (quilters and nonquilters) or her family, she continues to gather inspiration and give back.

Visit Jen's website at bettycrockerass.com.

JEN…ON INSPIRATION

I try to capture inspiration any way I can. I always have a small notebook and camera in hand. I have folders of print ads or things from magazines that sparked an idea, as well as files on my computer of screen shots and quick sketches. When I'm in a rut, I'll go through them and try to find that spark again.

> " I love supporting people practicing the "lost arts," as I like to call them. I feel that, with my own craft of bookbinding too, when you give someone something that special, even if you've been compensated for your time, your art becomes a piece of family history. Every time I see the quilt, I will think of Jen and how much love she has put into the quilt.
>
> —Eréne (Jen's friend)

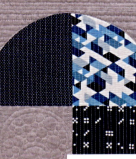

EVERY DAY

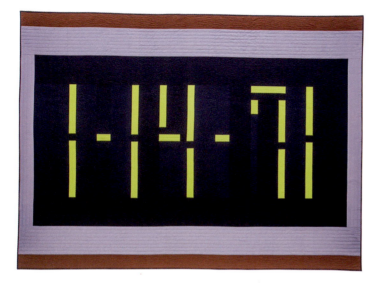

INSPIRATION

"Kevin, Amanda Jean's husband, proposed this quilt to her years ago, but she could never quite get excited by the idea. Inspired by a digital clock radio, he thought it was a fun idea that could be made very personal by individual quilters by using a meaningful date instead of a time. Amanda Jean needed to visualize it herself before she found the excitement. One night they were watching *Groundhog Day* and she finally caught the vision.

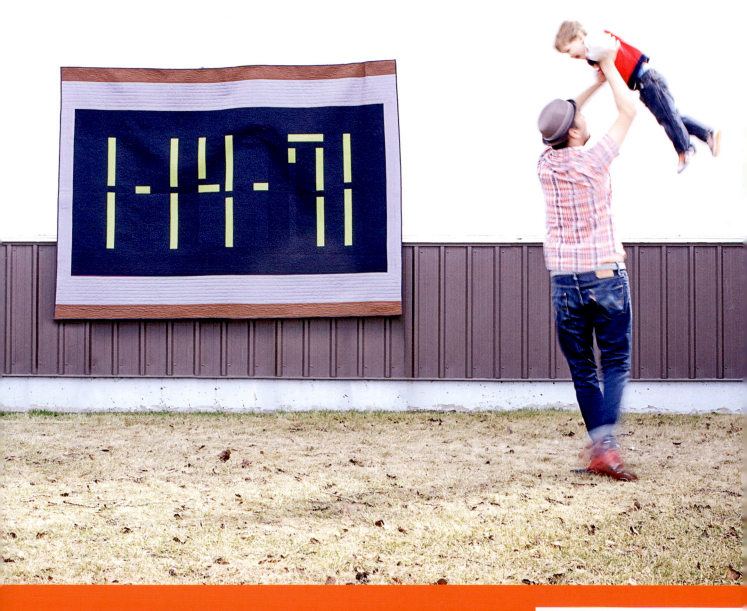

"

On a digital clock the dashes in the numbers are angled in the corners, so I was trying to come up with a way to make that work. I spent an entire night tossing and turning, subconsciously trying to figure out how to design the numbers. In the morning I got out some graph paper and did some sketching. It wasn't long before I switched to designing the numbers in Adobe Illustrator. Using the computer allowed me to make adjustments easily and quickly. In the end, I skipped the angled corners and made my own stylized version of digital numbers.

—*Amanda Jean (the designer)*

PROCESS

After that sleepless night and a bit more time on the computer, Amanda Jean shared the initial design with Kevin. There was some discussion together on color variations, but otherwise she made the quilt according to the initial sketch.

Patterns for the numerals 0–9 (pages 66 and 67) are included so you can personalize the quilt. Take it a step further by choosing colors that are meaningful to you.

AMANDA JEAN ... ON INSPIRATION

I take a lot of photos with my phone. It can be useful to capture a color scheme, an idea, or a design when I am out and about. I jot down notes on any scrap of paper I can find ... usually on the back of a grocery store receipt. On a good day, these sketches will get taped or transferred into one of my sketchbooks.

Photos by Amanda Jean Nyberg

Amanda Jean Nyberg

DATE STAMP

FINISHED BLOCKS: 2″ × 32″ | 4″ × 32″ | 10″ × 32″

FINISHED QUILT: 98″ × 72″

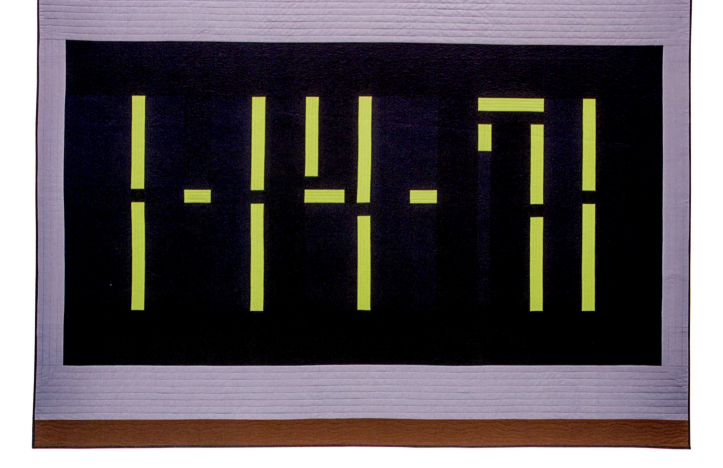

Materials Required

- **Dark gray (Kona Pepper):** 4⅓ yards for background
- **Green (Kona Chartreuse):** ⅔ yard for numbers
- **Gray (Kona Medium Gray):** 2 yards for inner borders
- **Brown (Kona Cappuccino):** ¾ yard for outer borders
- **Backing fabric:** 6 yards (pieced crosswise)
- **Binding fabric:** ⅞ yard
- **Batting:** 102˝ × 76˝

NOTE

*These instructions are more of a guide than an exact pattern. **Please keep in mind that the quilt you make may vary in size from the finished quilt shown.** Because of the combinations of numbers you may use, it is likely that you will need longer horizontal borders. Cut your pieces accordingly and adjust your batting and binding amounts. The materials list includes extra yardage to reflect this. Don't be alarmed if you have extra fabric at the end of your quilt project. You can use the extra to piece a creative quilt backing or use some of it for binding.*

Cutting Instructions

WOF = width of fabric

DARK GRAY:

- Cut 2 pieces 10½˝ × 32½˝ for the side background pieces.
- Cut 5 strips 8½˝ × WOF for the top and bottom background pieces.
- Cut the remaining pieces for numbers and spacers according to the chart (page 62) as needed.

GREEN:

- Cut 8 strips 2½˝ × WOF for the numbers.

GRAY:

- Cut 3 strips 4½˝ × WOF for the side borders.
- Cut 5 strips 8½˝ × WOF for the top and bottom borders.

BROWN:

- Cut 5 strips 4½˝ × WOF for the outer top and bottom borders.

BINDING FABRIC:

- Cut 10 strips 2½˝ × WOF.

Number-Specific Cutting Instructions

Numeral	Numbers fabric (green)	Background fabric (dark gray)
1	2½˝ × 14½˝ 2½˝ × 16½˝	2½˝ × 2½˝
2	2½˝ × 8½˝ 4 pieces 2½˝ × 10½˝	4 pieces 2½˝ × 2½˝ 8½˝ × 12½˝ 8½˝ × 14½˝
3	2½˝ × 8½˝ 4 pieces 2½˝ × 10½˝	4 pieces 2½˝ × 2½˝ 8½˝ × 12½˝ 8½˝ × 14½˝
4	2½˝ × 6½˝ 2½˝ × 12½˝ 2½˝ × 14½˝ 2½˝ × 16½˝	3 pieces 2½˝ × 2½˝ 6½˝ × 14½˝ 8½˝ × 16½˝
5	2½˝ × 8½˝ 4 pieces 2½˝ × 10½˝	4 pieces 2½˝ × 2½˝ 8½˝ × 12½˝ 8½˝ × 14½˝
6	2½˝ × 8½˝ 5 pieces 2½˝ × 10½˝	6 pieces 2½˝ × 2½˝ 6½˝ × 14½˝ 8½˝ × 12½˝
7	2½˝ × 4½˝ 2½˝ × 10½˝ 2½˝ × 12½˝ 2½˝ × 14½˝	3 pieces 2½˝ × 2½˝ 2½˝ × 24½˝ 6½˝ × 30½˝
8	2 pieces 2½˝ × 8½˝ 5 pieces 2½˝ × 10½˝	8 pieces 2½˝ × 2½˝ 6½˝ × 12½˝ 6½˝ × 14½˝
9	2 pieces 2½˝ × 8½˝ 4 pieces 2½˝ × 10½˝	6 pieces 2½˝ × 2½˝ 6½˝ × 12½˝ 8½˝ × 14½˝
0	4 pieces 2½˝ × 10½˝ 2 pieces 2½˝ × 12½˝	6 pieces 2½˝ × 2½˝ 6½˝ × 28½˝
Dash	2½˝ × 4½˝	4½˝ × 14½˝ 4½˝ × 16½˝
Spacers		6½˝ × 32½˝ each

ASSEMBLY

Make the Number Blocks

1. Determine what numbers you would like in your quilt. Think of a specific date or time, like your partner's birthday or the time a child was born.

2. Piece the number and sash blocks according to the assembly diagrams. Press in the direction of the arrows.

> **TIP**
>
> *Use your camera! It is a great way to evaluate your layout and spot problem areas or color clumping. It can give you a general idea of how your finished project will look before you sew it together. The photo can also be used as a reference if your blocks get shuffled out of order.*

AMANDA JEAN...ON TAKING OFF

Just jump right in and get sewing. Don't be afraid to make mistakes. Don't get hung up on perfectionism. (That's for everyone, whether you've made one quilt or 200 quilts.)

Assemble the Quilt Top

1. Arrange the blocks. Place spacer pieces between the numbers and between the numbers and the dashes. You may need as few as 5 or as many as 7 spacers. *Do not place spacers to the left of the first number or to the right of the last number.*

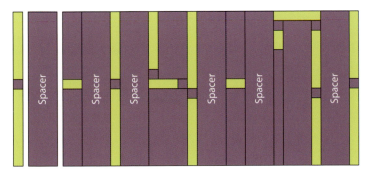

Numbers and spacers assembly

2. Sew the numbers and spacers together. Press the seams toward the spacers.

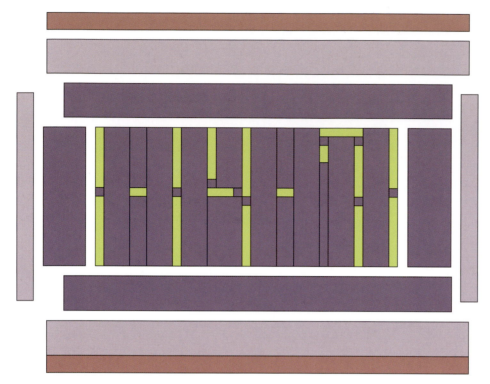

TIP

If your quilt center is wider than 78˝, you will need to adjust the length of the top and bottom borders.

Quilt assembly

3. Sew the 10½˝ × 32½˝ background fabric pieces to the sides of the quilt top. Press the seams away from the center.

TIP

To prevent wavy borders, measure and cut the border pieces accurately; then pin, pin, pin. Place the 2 layers together. Start by placing a pin on each end and a pin in the middle. Next, place pins at the midpoints of those 2 sections. Continue to place pins in the middle of each section until you have pinned every 6˝–8˝. Finally, sew carefully, easing in any bulk as you go.

4. Sew 5 strips 8½˝ × WOF of background fabric together end to end. Press the seams to one side. Cut 2 pieces to the width of your quilt. Pin and sew to the top and bottom of the quilt top. Press the seams away from the center.

5. Sew 3 strips 4½˝ × WOF of inner border fabric together end to end. Press the seams to one side. Cut 2 pieces 4½˝ × 48½˝. Pin and sew to the sides of the quilt top. Press the seams toward the border.

6. Sew 5 strips 8½˝ × WOF of inner border fabric together end to end. Press the seams to one side. Cut 2 pieces to the width of your quilt. Pin and sew to the top and bottom of the quilt top. Press the seams toward the border.

7. Sew 5 strips 4½˝ × WOF of outer border fabric together end to end. Press the seams to one side. Cut 2 pieces to the width of your quilt. (This will be the same measurement as in Step 6.) Pin and sew to the top and bottom of the quilt top. Press the seams toward the border. Your quilt top is complete!

BINDING

Square up the quilt. Make and apply the binding; finish by hand or machine.

Almost anything goes for your binding fabric. You could extend the quilt design by using coordinating fabrics. Or you could play up the clock radio inspiration and use a wood-grain print to mix it up.

Finish the Quilt

1. Make the quilt backing.

2. Create a quilt sandwich by layering the pieced top, batting, and backing. Secure the sandwich together using your preferred method of basting to prevent shifting while you are quilting.

3. Quilt as desired by hand or machine. This design benefits from an angular pattern, whether you choose an allover pattern or highlight the numbers in one motif and the background or border in another.

AMANDA JEAN…ON CHALLENGES

I can only recall one time that I have ever given up on a quilt. I'm a finisher and stubborn to the end. I have learned to appreciate a quilt challenge, and some of my favorite quilts have come about as a result. I average about 25 completed quilts a year. That means I finish one quilt approximately every two weeks. I'll be the first to admit that it sounds a little bit excessive when you break it down like that.

NUMBER ASSEMBLY

Use these assembly diagrams to keep you on track when sewing and pressing the number blocks. Note that the lower portions of the blocks are longer than the top portions.

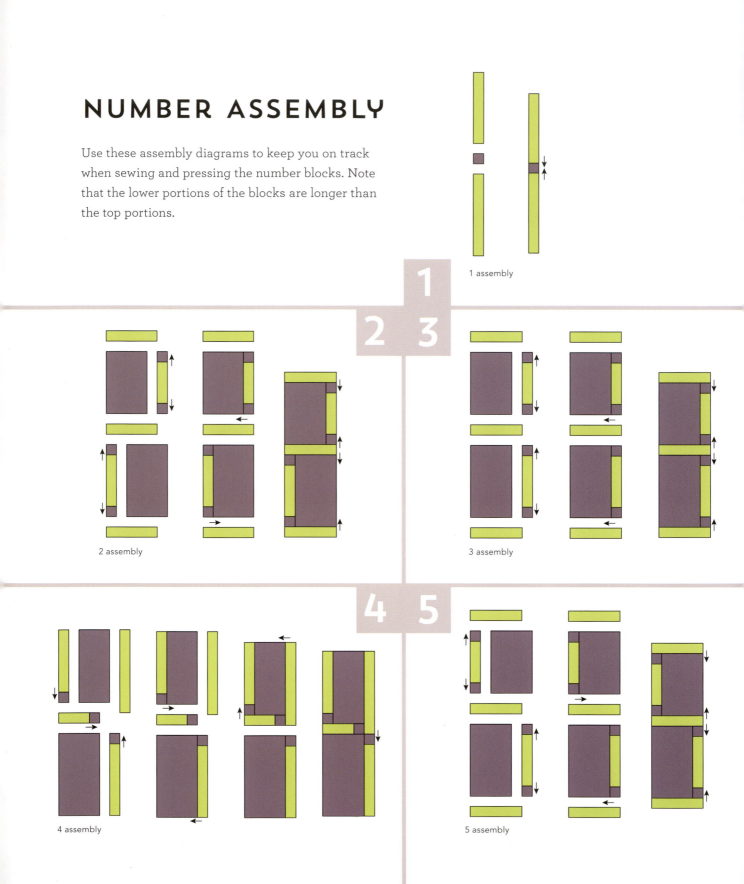

1 assembly

2 assembly

3 assembly

4 assembly

5 assembly

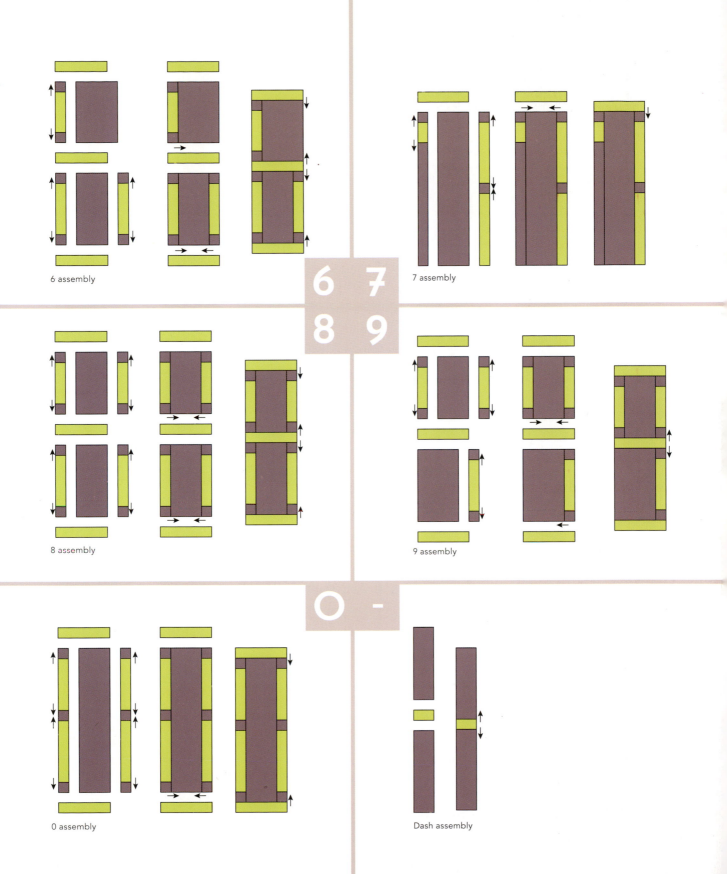

6 assembly

7 assembly

8 assembly

9 assembly

0 assembly

Dash assembly

QUILTMAKER
Amanda Jean Nyberg

Photo by Amanda Jean Nyberg

There is probably no quilter in the world today more obsessed with scraps than Amanda Jean. She can create from the tiniest bits, the stuff that the rest of us throw out for the squirrels.

Amanda Jean is a devoted friend, mother, and wife. Family will always be her most important priority, even when faced with deadlines. Thankfully, they all appreciate her career and the benefits of living with a quilter during the Minnesota winters.

Working out of her family home, Amanda Jean uses the lakeside location, her family, and nearly everything in the world around her as inspiration. Shapes, colors, and joy all come to her work. Self-taught and quilting for 15 years now, she has seen the first fabric she bought make its way into no less than eight different quilts! She tries to waste nothing.

Visit Amanda Jean's website at crazymomquilts.blogspot.com.

AMANDA JEAN … ON FAMILY

I'm very thankful that I get to quilt as a job. With my kids in school all day, I try to use my weekdays as efficiently as possible. In theory my workday would end when they walk through the door, but that isn't always the case. I make sure to cook dinner each night, because that is the one time of the day where we are all together in the same place at the same time. That family time is very important to us. Cleaning and laundry get squeezed in whenever I can find the time (or the energy).

NOSTALGIA, ALL WRAPPED UP

INSPIRATION

"Growing up in Montreal, my husband, Trent, and his family were appropriately hockey obsessed. Saturday night meant a fire in the fireplace and the family all together, watching the Montreal Canadiens on *Hockey Night in Canada*. When it came to this quilt, Trent wanted to evoke those memories and the pride of those Saturday nights. He asked for a hockey rink with a maple leaf on it. Ugh. Really? A hockey quilt? Ugh. How tacky. I can't do any NHL or Hockey Canada logo designs because they are copyrighted and trademarked. How many times did I have to tell him? I cannot do NHL logos. I cannot do Hockey Canada—it's trademark infringement. Was he not listening to me? And no, I won't use that hockey puck fabric!

—*Andrea (the designer)*

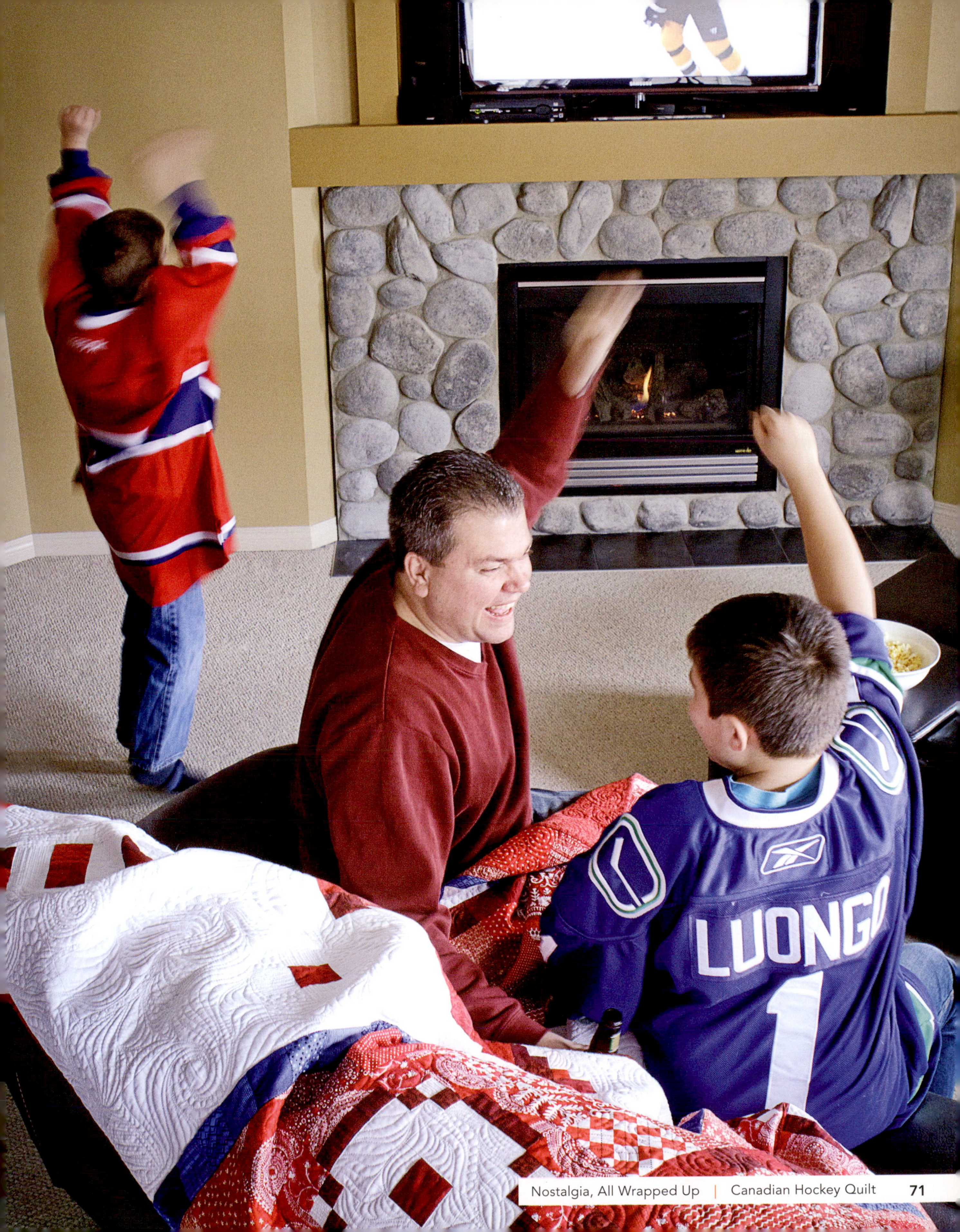
LUONGO
1

PROCESS

Andrea was less than enthused about the hockey idea. Frankly, she thought it was tacky. She spent endless hours researching hockey art, quotes, classic photographs, and old Montreal Canadiens paraphernalia. She played with some ideas incorporating colors and abstract images. Then she showed Trent. Her designs were intricate and abstract. He wanted something simple and sentimental.

In the end, he asked for a hockey rink with a maple leaf on it, and she provided that. No surprise, really—it fits well with Andrea's strong graphic sensibilities.

This quilt is scrap friendly—the greater the variety of prints used, the more interest in the finished quilt.

ANDREA … ON IMPROV

Improv is intimidating to me. I have not yet been able to explore it enough. I gasp at the gorgeous work and remain in my squares-and-rectangles style. I will venture out of my "box" soon enough.

NOTE

Not everyone is a Canadian hockey fan, or any type of hockey fan for that matter. So the following are some tips and ideas you can use to modify this pattern into a theme or symbol of your choice. The great thing about this type of design is that by using graph paper, you can design just about anything you want.

You can find a wealth of inspiration on the Internet just by using search engines and Pinterest. Coloring books, cross-stitch, and knitting patterns often have images online with shapes or objects already in grid form. Example keywords to help you in your search might include the following:

cross-stitch • pattern • mosaic • coloring book • motif • pixel (+ theme word or words)

IMPORTANT: It's important to be aware of the copyright on anything you might want to use from a book or from the Internet. If you see a design for a rose and it prompts you to create a design for daisies—no problem. But if you want to use the original rose design, you need to get permission from the original designer (or whoever holds the copyright).

There are also many pixilation tutorials online that you can use with your own photos and more sophisticated images.

Using graph paper, block off:
  40 × 32 squares (1 square = 1˝) or
  20 × 16 squares (1 square = 2˝).

Start sketching and filling in your desired shape. You can then fill in the rest of the squares of the graph paper to customize size, colors, and so on.

Andrea Harris

CANADIAN HOCKEY QUILT

FINISHED BLOCKS: 2˝ × 2˝ | 4˝ × 4˝ | 8˝ × 8˝ | 12˝ × 12˝ | 40˝ × 16˝ | 40˝ × 32˝

FINISHED QUILT: 96˝ × 64˝

Materials Required

- **Red and white print fabrics:** 3 yards total for side panels, goal blocks, and circle blocks

- **White-on-white fabrics:** 2¾ yards total for goal and circle blocks, maple leaf block, and center panel top and bottom

- **Dark red tonal fabrics (red prints without white):** 1½ yards total for circle blocks, lines, maple leaf block, and center panel top and bottom

- **Blue print fabrics:** ½ yard total for goal blocks and lines

TIP

When choosing your fabrics, don't hesitate to raid your scrap bin. Ideally, you will have at least 5–7 different fabrics in each colorway to maximize the variety in the quilt.

- **Backing fabric:** 6 yards (pieced crosswise)
- **Binding fabric:** ¾ yard
- **Batting:** 100˝ × 68˝

Cutting Instructions

WOF = width of fabric

RED AND WHITE PRINT FABRICS:

- Cut 20 strips 4½˝ × WOF.

  Subcut 19 strips into 152 squares 4½˝ × 4½˝ for the goal blocks and side panels.

  Subcut 1 strip into 16 rectangles 4½˝ × 2½˝ for the circle blocks.

- Cut 1 strip 2½˝ × WOF.

  Subcut 16 squares 2½˝ × 2½˝ for the circle blocks.

- Cut 3 strips 1½˝ × WOF.

  Subcut 1 strip into 2 rectangles 1½˝ × 8½˝ and 4 rectangles 1½˝ × 3½˝ for the goal blocks.

  Subcut 2 strips into 16 rectangles 1½˝ × 4½˝ for the circle blocks.

WHITE-ON-WHITE FABRICS:

- Cut 14 strips 4½˝ × WOF.

  Subcut 1 strip into 10 rectangles 4½˝ × 2½˝ for the goal and circle blocks.

  Subcut 1 strip into 8 rectangles 4½˝ × 3½˝ for the circle blocks.

  Subcut 12 strips into 92 squares 4½˝ × 4½˝ for the maple leaf block and center panel top and bottom.

- Cut 8 strips 2½˝ × WOF.

  Subcut 7 strips into 108 squares 2½˝ × 2½˝ for the maple leaf block and center panel top and bottom.

  Subcut 1 strip into 26 rectangles 2½˝ × 1½˝ for the circle and maple leaf blocks.

- Cut 3 strips 1½˝ × WOF.

  Subcut into 56 squares 1½˝ × 1½˝ for the circle and maple leaf blocks.

DARK RED TONAL FABRICS:

- Cut 14 strips 2½˝ × WOF.

  Subcut 13 strips into 198 squares 2½˝ × 2½˝ for the circle blocks, lines, maple leaf block, and center panel top and bottom.

  Subcut 1 strip into 26 rectangles 2½˝ × 1½˝ for the maple leaf block.

- Cut 4 strips 1½˝ × WOF.

  Subcut 3 strips into 56 squares 1½˝ × 1½˝ for the circle and maple leaf blocks.

  Subcut 1 strip into 16 rectangles 1½˝ × 4½˝ for the circle blocks.

BLUE PRINT FABRICS:

- Cut 4 strips 2½˝ × WOF.

  Subcut into 64 squares 2½˝ × 2½˝ for the blue lines.

- Cut 1 strip 1½˝ × WOF.

  Subcut into 2 rectangles 1½˝ × 4½˝ and 4 rectangles 1½˝ × 3½˝ for the goal blocks.

BINDING FABRIC:

- Cut 9 strips 2½˝ × WOF.

ASSEMBLY

Press all the seams open.

NOTE

Breaking down the design into blocks before sewing it together makes a seemingly complex design straightforward. But make sure you label your blocks as you go to avoid confusion when you begin assembling the quilt top.

Make the Goal Blocks

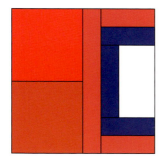

Goal block

1. Sew a blue rectangle 1½˝ × 4½˝ to a long side of a white rectangle 2½˝ × 4½˝. Sew blue rectangles 1½˝ × 3½˝ to the short sides.

2. Sew red print rectangles 1½˝ × 3½˝ to the short sides of the piece from Step 1. Sew a red print rectangle 1½˝ × 8½˝ to the long side of the block, as shown.

3. Sew 2 red print squares 4½˝ × 4½˝ together. Join to the piece from the previous step to complete the goal block.

4. Repeat Steps 1–3 to make 2 goal blocks. Set aside.

Make the Circle Blocks

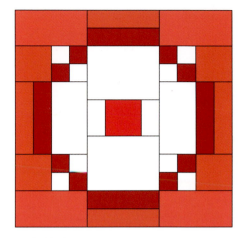

Circle block

1. Sew a dark red square 1½˝ × 1½˝ to a white square 1½˝ × 1½˝. Make 8. Sew 2 of these units together to make a Four-Patch unit. Repeat to make 4 Four-Patch units.

2. Arrange and sew a red print square 2½˝ × 2½˝ to each Four-Patch unit, noting the placement. Add a red print rectangle 2½˝ × 4½˝ to the Four-Patch unit. Repeat to make 4 units.

3. Sew a dark red rectangle 1½˝ × 4½˝ to a red print rectangle 1½˝ × 4½˝. Make 4. Sew 2 white rectangles 2½˝ × 4½˝ to the dark red sides of 2 of these pieces.

4. Sew 2 white rectangles 1½˝ × 2½˝ to the sides of the dark red square 2½˝ × 2½˝. Sew 2 white rectangles 3½˝ × 4½˝ to the top and bottom.

5. Arrange and sew the pieces together to make the circle block. Make 4. Set aside.

Make the Red Print Line

Make 2 rows of 16 squares 4½˝ × 4½˝ each. Chainstitch the squares into pairs; then sew together into groups of 4, 8, and finally 2 rows of 16 each. Set aside.

Make the Red Print Combo Blocks

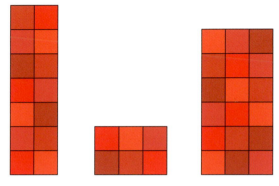

Red print squares assembly

1. Sew red print squares 4½˝ × 4½˝ together into pairs. Add additional single squares to make the following groupings:

4 combo blocks 2 × 7

---

4 combo blocks 2 × 3

---

2 combo blocks 3 × 6

2. Sew 2 × 7 red print combo blocks to the top and bottom of a goal block. Make 2. Set aside.

3. Sew a 3 × 6 red print combo block between 2 circle blocks. Make 2. Sew a 2 × 3 red print combo block to the top and bottom of the circle/combo block row. Make 2. Set aside.

Make the Dark Red Line

Make 2 rows of 32 squares 2½˝ × 2½˝ each. Chainstitch the squares into pairs; then sew together into groups of 4, 8, 16, and finally 2 rows of 32 each. Set aside.

Make the Blue Line

Make 2 rows of 32 squares 2½˝ × 2½˝ each. Chainstitch the squares into pairs; then sew together into groups of 4, 8, 16, and finally 2 rows of 32. Set aside.

Make the Maple Leaf Block

Construct the following blocks with dark red and white-on-white fabric to make the maple leaf block. Use 32 white squares 4½˝ × 4½˝ for the background. After you have made the blocks, arrange them and the background squares on your design wall according to the diagram (below). Some blocks are rotated a quarter-turn as indicated by the arrows in the block placement diagram. Arrange and sew into 8 rows of 10 blocks and squares each. Join the rows.

				H2	H1				
			G2	B2 →	B1 ←	G1			
	F2	E2	D2	L	L	D1	E1	F1	
	C2	L	A2 ←	L	L	A1 →	L	C1	
	B2	L	L	L	L	L	L	B1	
		A2	L	L	L	L	A1		
		H2	L	L	L	L	H1		
		I →	J	K →	K	J	I		

Block placement

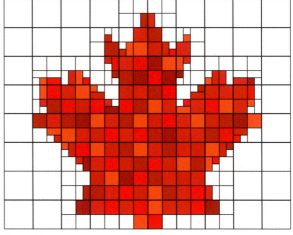

Assembly

BLOCKS A1 AND A2

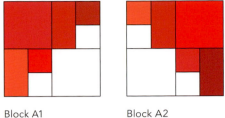

Block A1   Block A2

Make 2 of each.

4 red squares 2½″ × 2½″

4 white squares 2½″ × 2½″

8 red rectangles 1½″ × 2½″

8 red squares 1½″ × 1½″

8 white squares 1½″ × 1½″

BLOCKS B1 AND B2

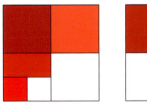

Block B1   Block B2

Make 2 of each.

8 red squares 2½″ × 2½″

4 white squares 2½″ × 2½″

4 red rectangles 1½″ × 2½″

4 red squares 1½″ × 1½″

4 white squares 1½″ × 1½″

BLOCKS C1 AND C2

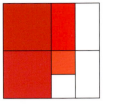
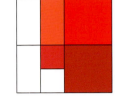

Block C1   Block C2

Make 1 of each.

4 red squares 2½″ × 2½″

4 white rectangles 1½″ × 2½″

2 red rectangles 1½″ × 2½″

2 white squares 1½″ × 1½″

2 red squares 1½″ × 1½″

BLOCKS D1 AND D2

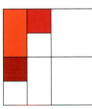
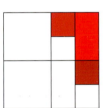

Block D1   Block D2

Make 1 of each.

4 white squares 2½″ × 2½″

2 white rectangles 1½″ × 2½″

2 red rectangles 1½″ × 2½″

4 red squares 1½″ × 1½″

4 white squares 1½″ × 1½″

BLOCKS E1 AND E2

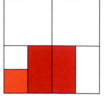 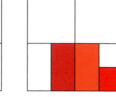

Block E1   Block E2

Make 1 of each.

4 white squares 2½˝ × 2½˝

2 white rectangles 1½˝ × 2½˝

4 red rectangles 1½˝ × 2½˝

2 white squares 1½˝ × 1½˝

2 red squares 1½˝ × 1½˝

BLOCKS G1 AND G2

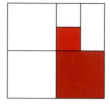 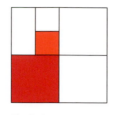

Block G1   Block G2

Make 1 of each.

4 white squares 2½˝ × 2½˝

2 red squares 2½˝ × 2½˝

2 white rectangles 1½˝ × 2½˝

2 white squares 1½˝ × 1½˝

2 red squares 1½˝ × 1½˝

BLOCKS F1 AND F2

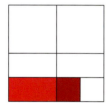 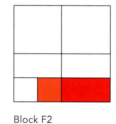

Block F1   Block F2

Make 1 of each.

4 white squares 2½˝ × 2½˝

4 white rectangles 1½˝ × 2½˝

2 red rectangles 1½˝ × 2½˝

2 red squares 1½˝ × 1½˝

2 white squares 1½˝ × 1½˝

BLOCKS H1 AND H2

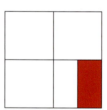 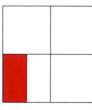

Block H1   Block H2

Make 2 of each.

12 white squares 2½˝ × 2½˝

4 white rectangles 1½˝ × 2½˝

4 red rectangles 1½˝ × 2½˝

BLOCK I

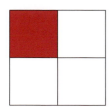

Block I

Make 22. (Set aside 20 for the center panel top and bottom.)

66 white squares 2½˝ × 2½˝

22 red squares 2½˝ × 2½˝

BLOCK J

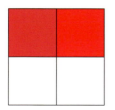

Block J

Make 2.

4 red squares 2½˝ × 2½˝

4 white squares 2½˝ × 2½˝

BLOCK K

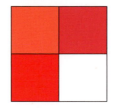

Block K

Make 2.

6 red squares 2½˝ × 2½˝

2 white squares 2½˝ × 2½˝

BLOCK L

Block L

Make 20.

80 red squares 2½˝ × 2½˝

ANDREA…ON DESIGN

I was always interested in geometric designs and patterns growing up, and when I saw them paired with the bold colors and eye candy of a fabric shop…I fell hard!

My first quilt was based on a Rail Fence design. After I got the basics of how to make a quilt, my mind started to take off with all sorts of ideas of graphic patterns. When I design, I use only black and white. That's how I see the pattern. I add the color later on.

Make the Center Panel Top

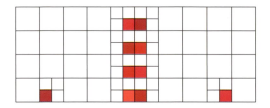

Center panel top assembly

Assemble 30 white squares 4½˝ × 4½˝ and 10 I blocks together according to the center panel top assembly diagram (above). Note the slight difference in placement of the 2 lower I blocks.

Make the Center Panel Bottom

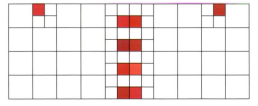

Center panel bottom assembly

Assemble 30 white squares 4½˝ × 4½˝ and 10 I blocks together according to the center panel bottom assembly diagram (above). Note the slight difference in placement of the 2 upper I blocks.

Assemble the Quilt Top

1. Sew the center panel top to the maple leaf block.

2. Sew the center panel bottom to the maple leaf block.

3. Assemble the quilt top according to the quilt assembly diagram (below).

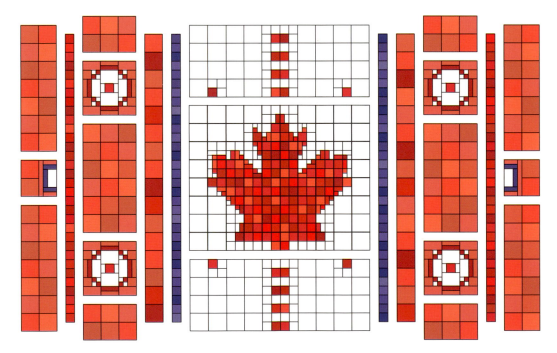

Quilt assembly

Finish the Quilt

1. Make the quilt backing.

2. Create a quilt sandwich by layering the pieced top, batting, and backing. Secure the sandwich together using your preferred method of basting to prevent shifting while you are quilting.

3. If you desire, you can emphasize the hockey theme with your quilting. Andrea used circle templates to enhance the face-off circles. Then she chose denser quilting for the white of the quilt to make the center maple leaf pop. The goal block was quilted in a diamond pattern, with a casual goal "crease" in front.

> **TIP**
>
> *It is easier to mark the quilt for quilting before you baste it.*

BINDING

Square up the quilt. Make and apply the binding; finish by hand or machine.

Trent could not be happier with the final quilt. He anticipates many more Saturday nights on the couch watching hockey—this time with his boys (and a beer, of course). He already anticipates an emotional reaction.

ANDREA...ON TEACHING

My favorite part of teaching is connecting with those students who are apprehensive and unsure of their abilities. Often students feel intimidated by experienced quilters. They make many excuses and wavering comments at the beginning of a session, but then start to relax and make jokes. Seeing their big smiles at the end is priceless.

QUILTMAKER
Andrea Harris

Any quilter with kids knows the struggle to balance family and creativity. Andrea Harris is no different. But ask her which she will put aside and it will always be the quilting, no matter how inspired or motivated she feels. She is driven and excited by her family, and that passion shines through in her quilting.

Andrea is a quilt designer and longarm quilter. She has the ability to think in black and white in her quilts, always starting with graphic design, and bringing in color and fabrics only after the design elements are confirmed. It isn't a common approach, but it works really well for her. It also gives her the chance to design and play in the midst of a busy life.

On top of her quilting, Andrea is a mom to two school-aged boys and a wife to Trent. Don't forget the dog and cat in the family too. A teacher in her previous life, she is happily home quilting during the school day and scheming ways to bring even more fun into a laughter-filled household.

Visit Andrea's website at urbanquiltworks.com.

ANDREA…ON FLOW

I like the quiet and solitude of my quilting hobby and am glad to have something that is all my own. Sometimes it is hard to balance housework, groceries, errands, kid schedules, and quilting. When I focus on one, the other goes off-balance. I always feel like one (quilting) or the other (house or kids) is off-balance.

> It's like a childhood teddy bear or Linus' blanket—a tradition. A quilt that my beautiful, wonderful wife has put her blood, sweat, and tears into for me, knowing she had no interest in making it for me, as the design is not aligned to her usual creative ways. This quilt will have an emotional connection—no, I'm serious; I'll cry.
>
> —Trent (Andrea's husband)

CREATIVE COMBINATIONS

INSPIRATION

"The idea for this quilt came from Peter, Blair's husband. He is also a creative soul who pushes Blair to think outside the box.

Initially Blair thought a ski jacket quilt was another one of Peter's wacky and unconventional ideas. In her words, he is "the 'pie-in-the-sky' idea guy, and I am the more practical voice, looking at appropriate, compatible fabrics." Creatively, it is a combination that works.

PROCESS

In addition to picking the parka fabrics together, Blair and Peter collaborated on the design. Because both of them are visual people who, in Blair's words, "usually come to the same idea from a completely different place," they sat down together to sketch. This helped them be clear on the intention and design of the piece.

Peter is happy to live in a house with only one quilter. His pride in her career and creativity is evident. (Not to mention that her quilts keep him warm.)

BLAIR...ON INSPIRATION

Whenever I feel creatively stuck, I try to take a field trip and go to a park, a museum, even a shopping area with beautiful windows. My camera on my phone is indispensible. I also tear pages from interiors magazines and collect vintage quilting and craft books. I love painting and sketching and often will turn to that just to change things up creatively.

Photos by Blair Stocker

BLAIR STOCKER

SKI PARKA QUILT

FINISHED BLOCK: 9˝ × 9˝

FINISHED QUILT: 36˝ × 54˝

Materials Required

- **Warm colors (orange, yellow, pink):** at least 4 ski parkas
- **Cool colors (blue, green, gray):** at least 4 ski parkas
- **Backing fabric:** 1¾ yards
- **Packaged ½˝ piping (orange):** 6 yards
- **Batting (low loft):** 40˝ × 58˝

Cutting Instructions

Cut the ski parkas into usable panels by cutting them apart at the side seams and armholes and cutting away the collar and front zipper. Consider using the pockets in a few squares; those details can add a lot of interest to the surface of the quilt.

WARM COLORS:

- Cut 6 squares 10˝ × 10˝ for half-square triangle blocks.
- Cut 4 squares 9½˝ × 9½˝ for square blocks.

COOL COLORS:

- Cut 6 squares 10˝ × 10˝ for half-square triangle blocks.
- Cut 8 squares 9½˝ × 9½˝ for square blocks.

BLAIR…ON FLOW

Getting an inspired idea down on paper is energizing. After the fabrics are selected and the repetitive cutting process begins, I will listen to audiobooks or watch movies in my studio (I'm a big horror movie fan). The sewing and patchwork requires yet another type of focus. The final stage, the binding, is when I can sit with my family and hand stitch. Each part is satisfying in its own way. I think that's what I love about quiltmaking: just when you feel you can't do one more (when cutting, piecing, and so on), you move on to the next part and it all changes again.

ASSEMBLY

Make the Half-Square Triangle Blocks

Note: Use a sewing machine needle size 16/100 for these heavier fabrics.

TIP

Use a good-quality thread for your patch-work. It's worth spending a little more to buy a strong, fine, neutral-colored thread—your quilt will benefit from the strength.

1. Place a cool-colored square 10˝ × 10˝ on top of a warm-colored square 10˝ × 10˝, right sides together. Using a black pen and ruler, draw a straight line diagonally from corner to corner. Pin through both layers to hold the pieces in place. Using a walking foot, sew a generous ¼˝ away from either side of the drawn line. Cut through all the layers on the line to make 2 half-square triangle blocks. Repeat to make 12 half-square triangle blocks.

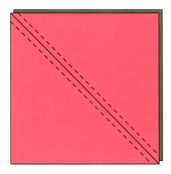

Half-square triangle construction

2. Open, but do not press. Square up each half-square triangle block to 9½˝ × 9½˝.

Assemble the Quilt Top

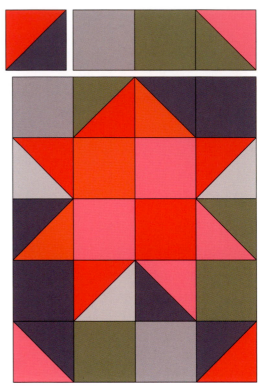

Quilt assembly

1. Arrange the quilt blocks following the quilt assembly diagram (above). Spread the colors around to have a good visual mix of warm and cool colors.

2. Sew the blocks into 6 rows of 4 blocks each. Again, use a generous ¼˝ seam allowance. It is helpful to use plenty of pins.

NOTE

Keep in mind that there is no easy way to press the seam allowances to one side or the other, but for this type of quilt it doesn't really matter. Actually, Blair didn't use the iron at all!

3. Join the rows together. Pin on either side of where the blocks meet to keep the points matching up well. Go slowly.

4. If necessary, trim to straighten the sides of the quilt.

Add Piping around the Quilt Edge

1. With the raw edges of the piping and the quilt together, and working on the right side of the quilt top, line up and pin the piping around the edges. Using a zipper or piping foot and thread that matches the piping, sew the piping onto the edge of the quilt top. Keep the stitching close to the piping.

2. Stop stitching a few inches away from the start. Use a seam ripper to open the ends of the piping. Trim the ends of the cording so they butt together closely. Fold a raw edge of the piping under ¼˝ and press. Overlap the piping fabric ends and trim the excess. With the folded edge covering the raw edge, pin into place and continue sewing. A stiletto is helpful for lining everything up.

> **TIP**
>
> *A bamboo stiletto helps guide the pieces through the sewing machine and helps keep the seam allowances flat and lined up.*

Finish the Quilt

1. Baste the batting and backing fabric together well. Do not baste the quilt top.

2. Place the basted batting and backing layers so that the backing is right side up on your work surface with the batting underneath. Lay the quilt top right side down on the backing/batting and pin through all the layers every 4˝ to secure.

3. Still using the piping or zipper foot, sew around all 4 edges of the quilt top, staying close to the stitching line for the piping. Leave a 10˝ opening on the bottom edge of the quilt.

4. Trim the batting and backing layers with pinking shears to be flush with the quilt top edges. Remove the basting stitches or pins.

5. Turn the entire piece right side out and gently push out all the corners. Close the 10˝ opening by folding in the edges and securing the opening with blind stitches.

6. To secure all 3 layers together, work from the front of the quilt and stitch a bar tack or several tight zigzag stitches at each point where 4 blocks meet. Use thread that blends in with the design (these bar tacks are not meant to add to the design itself, but simply to hold the layers together). Alternatively, you could tie the quilt.

QUILTMAKER

Blair Stocker

Photo by Blair Stocker

A Seattle-based quilter, painter, and writer, Blair runs her studio out of her home, which she shares with her creative husband and two teenagers.

The very first quilt Blair made was one created from her daughter's baby clothes. Like many new quilters, she was hooked on the process and the result without even having the skills in place. Designing her own quilts for five years now, Blair has a graphic aesthetic with a definite respect for tradition.

Blair paints when she isn't quilting. Using her creativity in other ways keeps her motivated and relaxed. With no patience to learn computer design programs, she turns to graph paper, colored pencils or watercolors, and her imagination to begin the transition from idea to quilt.

Visit Blair's website at wisecrafthandmade.com.

BLAIR…ON MAKING MISTAKES

Mistakes happen in every quilt, no matter how long you've quilted. Embrace these little (invisible to everyone but you) mistakes as part of the beauty of handmade quilts.

BLAIR…ON IMPROV

In my own work, I tend to prefer to be very structured. I love trying improv techniques because they get me out of my preconceived comfort zone. There's always something to be learned from being told to do things like put away our measuring tools and cut freehand or piece without preplanning.

> "At my parents' house in New Mexico, they have a large square piece of what looked like ski jacket quilted nylon fabric, embroidered all over with vivid colors. It looked warm and interesting. Because Blair works with a lot of repurposed fabrics, I thought it would be a cool idea to try.
>
> —Peter (Blair's husband)

LEARNING TO LOVE

INSPIRATION

"A lifelong gamer and fantasy reader, Rossie's husband, Jon, grew up loving maps. When he wasn't reading about fantastical places or immersed in a game that was as highly focused on a sense of place as it was on character, he sketched maps.

To get to the point of making a quilt, however, Jon had to bring Rossie into the world of these fantasy games. It was important to Jon that she understand the importance of the maps to the stories and games to which they belonged. And the quilt had to provide places for stories and adventures.

PROCESS

The design process was quite iterative between Rossie and Jon. Hexagons feature widely in many fantasy game maps, as do line drawings of features and places. After the hexagon was chosen as the basis of this quilt, Rossie proceeded with the design.

Rossie's favorite part of the quilting process is fabric selection and design wall work, so this project was well suited to her strengths. With the norms of fantasy game maps fed to her by Jon, they were able to choose fabrics.

For your own quilt, get to know your own game, your own story, and build the map to reflect the places it needs to include. For the quilter, getting lost in the fabric selection is the story, to some extent. For the recipient, the quilt is indeed the map to the story.

> **NOTE**
>
> *You don't have to be a lover of role-playing games to enjoy making or receiving this quilt. Make up your own fantasy. Focus on the storytelling aspect and it becomes a great family quilt.*

" After I had made a draft of the hexagon map in fabric on my design wall, I really wanted him to look at it. I had my story of the map—a village with a meadow surrounding it, then fields before you reach a walled castle, which has a city on the other side, and so on. I wanted to know if he saw it, too, and if it made sense to him. I didn't know if it would be a usable map. I didn't know if the map was too busy or not busy enough. There were some fabrics I wanted to pull for purely quilt-design reasons (not liking the play of color and value), and I didn't know if I should leave them for story.

Jon came to my studio one morning to look at the hexagons up on the design wall. I purposely didn't say anything about them, so that I could hear from him what immediately made sense and what didn't work. Together we pulled off some parts of the map and moved other pieces around. I had left a corner of the map blank, and we talked about how he would fill it. Then we went out for lunch!

—*Rossie (the designer)*

Photos by Rossie Hutchinson

ROSSIE HUTCHINSON

Quilted by Bernie Olszewski

GAMERS' HEX MAP

FINISHED QUILT: 68˝ × 79˝

Materials Required

- **Assorted prints:** 7½ yards for hexagons
- **Backing fabric:** 5 yards
- **Binding fabric:** ⅝ yard
- **Batting:** 72″ × 83″

Cutting Instructions

WOF = width of fabric

NOTE

Rossie cut all her fabric with a 4½″ hexagon die for the AccuQuilt GO! cutter. Accurately cutting the hexagons is the key to success on this project. You can, of course, make a template out of plastic or cardboard and cut the hexagons by hand or with a rotary cutter. Whatever method you use, be sure to press and starch your fabric before cutting and be as precise as possible when you are cutting.

PRINTS:

Enlarge, then trace or copy the pattern (page 105), and cut hexagons with 4½″ sides (resulting in hexagons that are approximately 9″ × 8″ including seam allowances). Or, use a die cutter.

- Cut a minimum of 115 whole hexagons.
- Cut 12 half-hexagons, ensuring that you add an extra ¼″ seam allowance to the center of each. Wait to cut these until you've determined the rest of the hexagon placements, as these are for the tops and bottoms of the rows. An option is to use half-hexagons within the quilt to change the lines.

TIP

Cut more hexagons than you think you will need. This gives you a chance to properly play around with the layout. Extra hexagons can be used to practice piecing or on the back.

BINDING FABRIC:

- Cut 8 strips 2″ × WOF.

FABRIC SELECTION AND PLACEMENT

When selecting fabric for your own map, consider the following:

- **Emphasize terrain.** Maps are heavy on terrain, not creatures.

- **Go plain.** There are usually a limited number of types of terrain in a map (maybe five), so there's no need to go wild finding a huge diversity of fabrics.

- **Color matters.** If possible, each type of terrain should have a unique color. For example, if water is blue, don't also have blue cities or blue forests.

- **Each hexagon matters.** For a gamer, a city can be marked by a single hex, because it is likely to come up in a story as "Go to the city of Elias and talk to the merchant!" rather than as an extensive city to traverse.

- **Scale isn't important.** Don't worry if the trees in your forest are twice the size of the mountains in your mountain fabric. These differences are of no consequence.

- **Leave things open-ended.** For example, Rossie placed a single hexagon of a pennant print in the middle of the meadows. She inserted this thinking that it was a training ground for soldiers from the castle. Jon thought that maybe it meant there was a treasure to be found in that spot. There are many ways to interpret that piece of the map, which is great! This sort of flexibility is useful for gamers as they tell their stories.

- **Consider typical geography.** In the real world, cities are usually built along waterways, castles have settlements near them, rivers flow into lakes, and meadows give way to forests. While this map is a fantasy, using some real-world principles to govern your fabric placement will help gamers make sense of it.

- **Follow the fabric.** This map contains a castle surrounded by walls largely because Rossie had that fabric and was dying to include it in the map. Once it was up on the design wall, she feared it occupied too much space, which Jon confirmed, but neither wanted to remove any part of it because it was so cool. If you find a unique fabric that you want to include, go for it! Your gamer can handle the unexpected.

- **Stretch the rules to suit your quilting needs.** This quilt has more types of terrain than a typical map. The castle and castle walls are huge and the city sprawls a bit. These features were not edited out because they made the map work as a quilt, in addition to working as a game board.

- **It takes more fabric than you think.** This particular quilt uses 19 different fabrics. Four were used for the dominant types of terrain (two green meadow fabrics, the darker water fabric, and the forest fabric) and required 1 yard each. For the rest, a ½-yard or fat quarter is generally sufficient.

ASSEMBLY

Assemble the Quilt Top

1. Using a design wall, lay out your quilt in a pleasing pattern. This quilt relies on 2 column styles:

Column A starts and finishes with half-hexagons and has 10 whole hexagons.

Column B has 11 whole hexagons.

> **NOTE**
>
> *No 2 quilts will be exactly the same. Use your fabric, your story, your game to inspire your own layout.*

2. Label the columns. Use masking tape to label the hexagons according to their placement in your quilt top. Give each column a letter and then number each hexagon in the column in descending order. Thus, the first column would be labeled A1, A2, A3, and so on.

> **TIP**
>
> *Set your stitch length smaller than you'd use for typical patchwork. A smaller stitch length will be useful for stopping the stitch line accurately. It also increases stitch strength—you'll be flipping parts of your piecing quite a bit before stitching over the ends.*

3. Piece the columns. Attach the bottom of hexagon A1 to the top of hexagon A2, the bottom of A2 to the top of A3, and so on, down the columns. Do not backstitch. Do not press. Join all the hexagons in each of the columns.

4. Join the columns. Position the columns so the 2 edges you are joining lie flat on top of each other, right sides together, with the edges and corners matching perfectly. Using a scant ¼″ seam, stitch the pieces together, starting and stopping ¼″ from the corners and backstitching for ¼″ or so. Do not sew over the seams you made in Step 3. It is important to stop and backstitch at the right spot—you can find it by eyeballing it or by using the seam already in the patchwork. You will have to reposition the columns for each short seam. The rest of the columns will be splayed off at what may seem like strange angles, but just focus on the line you need to stitch! Do not press as you join the columns.

5. Position the edges of the next hexagons on top of each other and arrange the rest of the columns so that they are out of the way. Sew the seam, starting and stopping ¼″ from the corners and backstitching.

6. Continue to sew the columns together. If you lose your place, simply lay out the columns to see where they need to be joined.

7. After all the columns have been joined, press the seams. Press the seams in each column up; press the seams between the columns open.

Finish the Quilt

1. Trim the sides of the quilt using a large straight ruler, rotary cutter, and cutting mat. You may choose to leave the full hexagons on the side, but you will have to bind around them.

2. Make the quilt backing.

3. Create a quilt sandwich by layering the pieced top, batting, and backing. Secure the sandwich together using your preferred method of basting to prevent shifting while you are quilting.

4. Quilt as desired. Rossie used a topographical pattern. Maybe try a straight-line grid or follow the lines of the hexagons.

BINDING

Make and apply the binding; finish by hand or machine.

Jon is thrilled with the quilt. As he puts it, "It felt like rolling a natural 20!" For a gamer, that's as good as it gets. And for Rossie, the quilter, the joy comes from creating something that her husband loves, more so than the pleasure and challenge of making the quilt itself.

**ROSSIE…
ON INSPIRATION**

I have a practiced laziness when it comes to inspirations. I tend to have too many ideas and find that not recording them helps reduce the clutter in my design brain. The right ones stick.

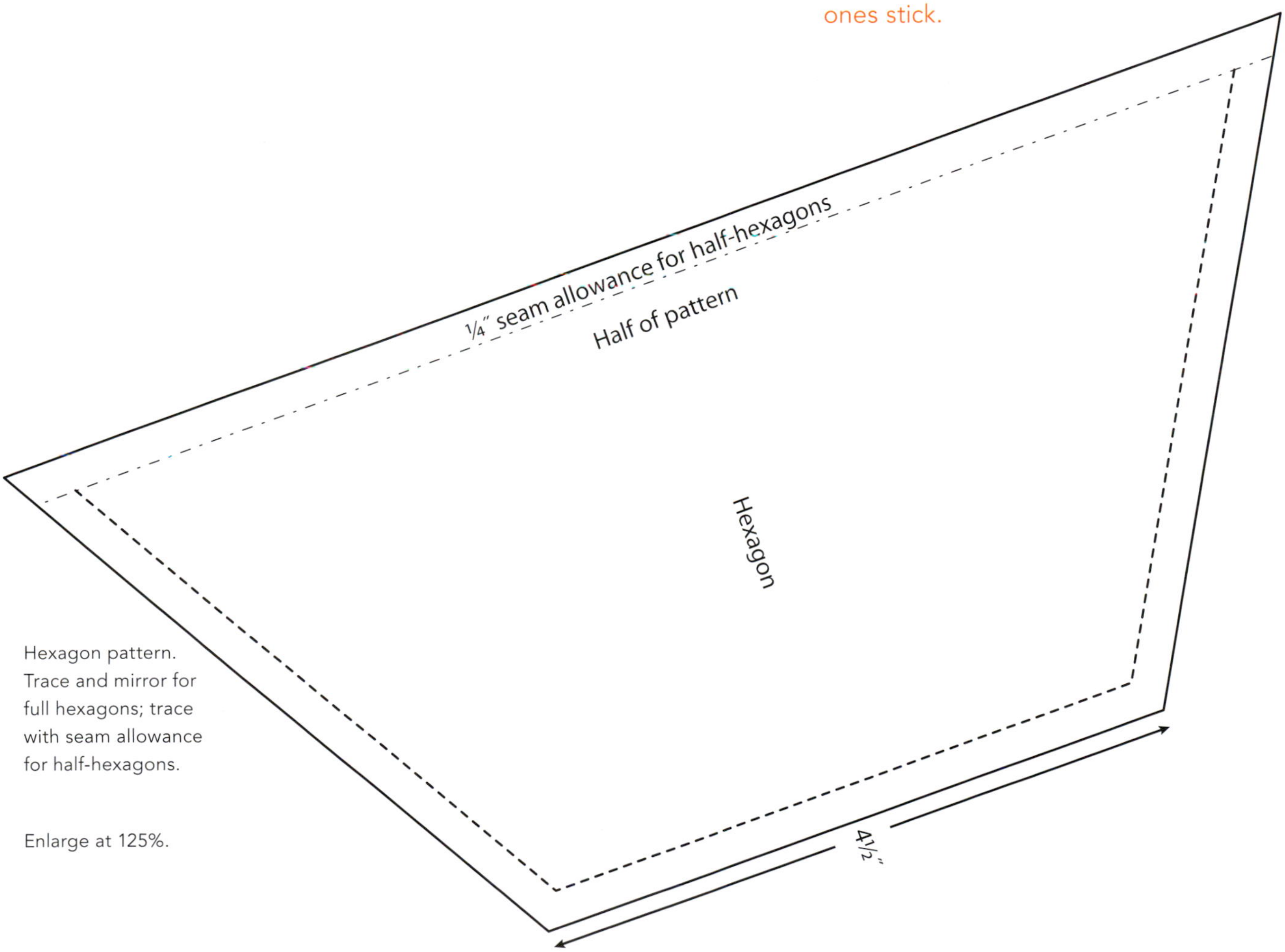

¼" seam allowance for half-hexagons

Half of pattern

Hexagon

Hexagon pattern. Trace and mirror for full hexagons; trace with seam allowance for half-hexagons.

Enlarge at 125%.

4½"

QUILTMAKER
Rossie Hutchinson

Photo by Emily Schildhouse

A professor by day and quilter by night, Rossie is the leader of the popular Flickr group Fresh Modern Quilts. She works to define modern quilting and pushes the online quilting community to examine and re-examine statements made in quilts and blog posts. Rossie is enthusiastic and supportive of creativity and of quilters who push the limits of what can be done. Her quilts are graphic, dynamic, and often likely to contain her favorite color: Kona Curry.

Married just since 2013, Rossie and Jon have a strong respect for their relationship to each other and to Rossie's quilting. She was a quilter before she met Jon, having started in 2003, and will always be a quilter. He is enthusiastic about her quilting because he sees Rossie as a rare individual who took her passion and turned it into her profession, while most of us are lucky if we can find our passion in our profession.

Working in a studio outside the home keeps them from falling over stacks of fabric. That's helpful with two rescue dogs in the house.

Visit Rossie's website at r0ssie.blogspot.com.

ROSSIE … ON CHALLENGES

When something isn't working for me, usually I just change course and try again, but if a quilt is still not working, I will donate my patchwork to a local charity that will happily finish it and give it to a worthy cause.

> "The geography was so important to the world it contained. As I've gotten older, I've searched for ways to make the maps even more special. I've drawn on parchment and leather, but this was the first time I've been able to inspire fabric telling the story of the map.
>
> —Jon (Rossie's husband)

PLAY DATE

INSPIRATION

Carolyn sat down with her three-year-old nephew Jacob and his brand-new baby brother one day to chat quilts. That lasted about two minutes. But in those two minutes Jacob talked about dinosaurs, as many a three-year-old boy is likely to do. When working with kids, it's hard to steer things the way we want them to go; instead, Carolyn embraced Jacob's idea and energy. It isn't an easy thing to do when you have a distinct style all your own, but it is significantly easier when you love the kid and all the time you spend together.

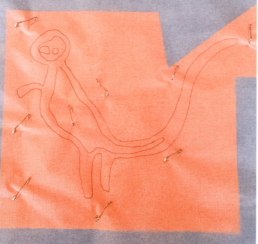

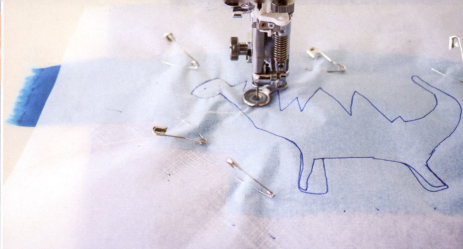

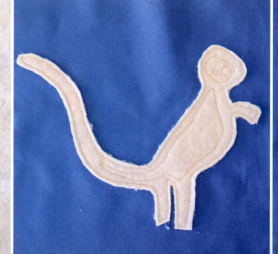

PROCESS

The first step in Carolyn and Jacob's collaboration was some painting. They only made it to two paintings before Jacob moved on to fabric selection. This is, arguably, his favorite part of playing with his aunt. From the paintings Carolyn created appliqué motifs. She followed his lead and embraced the notion of play with him.

This pattern is more of a guideline on the appliqué technique used. Play with your own nephew, kid, student, or cousin to create a personalized quilt. Draw or paint pictures and trace them to create the appliqués. Add or subtract blocks, or include blank blocks, to change the size of the quilt.

" At first, I was kind of thinking of a wholecloth approach with one big panel and appliquéing directly onto it. But I kind of like the idea of breaking it into blocks, because I like the feeling of the whole thing being a collection of drawings. In my mind, it could be a quilt made from the drawings and paintings that fill up your refrigerator if you have a kid and do that kind of thing. Plus, I thought that by breaking up the design into blocks, it would be more fun picking out fabrics and changing it up throughout.

—*Carolyn (the designer)*

Photos by Carolyn Friedlander

CAROLYN FRIEDLANDER

DINO PATCH

FINISHED BLOCK: 10˝ × 10˝

FINISHED QUILT: 48˝ × 60˝

Materials Required

- **Assorted prints:**

    1¾ yards total for backgrounds (2¼ yards if narrower than 42˝)

    1¾ yards total for appliqué shapes (2¼ yards if narrower than 42˝)

- **Border fabric:** 1¼ yards

- **Backing fabric:** 3⅛ yards (pieced crosswise)

- **Binding fabric:** ½ yard

- **Batting:** 52˝ × 64˝ plus 42˝ × 52½˝ for trapunto effect (*optional*)

- **Tracing paper**

Cutting

WOF = width of fabric

BACKGROUND FABRICS:

- Cut 20 squares 10½˝ × 10½˝ for the block backgrounds.

APPLIQUÉ FABRICS:

- Cut 20 squares 10½˝ × 10½˝ (or the size of your design) for the appliqués.

BATTING FOR TRAPUNTO (*OPTIONAL*):

- Cut 20 squares 10½˝ × 10½˝ (or the size of your design).

BORDER FABRIC:

- Cut 4 strips 4½˝ × WOF.

- Cut 2 strips 6½˝ × WOF.

BINDING FABRIC:

- Cut 6 strips 2½˝ × WOF.

CAROLYN … ON DESIGN

I was designing my own quilts from the very beginning. My first quilt was really just a means of including as many beautiful fabrics as possible and of getting something to the point where I could quilt it. Looking back, my first quilt had much more of a focus on the fabric and quilting rather than on the pieced design. As I learned more about how to piece, that part has played more of a role as well.

What you won't find me doing a lot of is any precise precutting or working with too many fancy rulers. I love paper piecing and appliqué because they allow me to be precise in other ways, and they let me jump into the sewing process sooner.

ASSEMBLY

Make the Blocks

1. Draw or paint pictures with your favorite little kid (or your second favorite). It is best to use a thick marker or paintbrush so a defined, thick line is available for tracing. Pick your favorite line drawings for the appliqués.

2. Use a piece of tracing paper, right side up, and trace the line drawings to create an appliqué design.

3. Layer the optional batting for trapunto, the background fabric, the appliqué fabric, and the traced design, all right sides up. Safety pin the layers together.

4. Using free-motion quilting or a straight stitch with a 2.0 stitch length, stitch on the traced lines, stitching right through the paper. Lock the first and last stitches in place with tiny stitches or backstitching.

5. After stitching all the areas, remove the tracing paper.

6. Use sharp scissors to trim away the excess appliqué fabric by cutting ⅛˝ away from the stitching lines. Be careful not to cut the background fabric or any stitching.

> **TIP**
>
> *Use a seam ripper at any tight places or in areas where you need to catch the top layer easily.*

7. If you are using the trapunto effect, trim from the back the trapunto batting near the outer stitching lines.

Assemble the Quilt Top

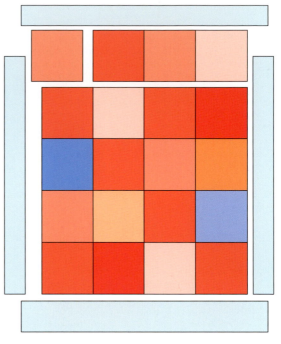

Quilt assembly

1. Arrange and sew the blocks into 5 rows of 4 blocks each.

2. Press the seams in alternating directions between the rows.

3. Join the rows together. Press the seams toward the bottom of the quilt.

4. Sew 4 strips of 4½˝ × WOF border fabric together end to end. Cut 2 pieces 4½˝ × 50½˝ for the side borders and 1 piece 4½˝ × 48½˝ for the top border. Sew 2 strips 6½˝ × WOF border fabric together end to end. Cut 1 piece 6½˝ × 48½˝ for the bottom border.

5. Sew the side borders to the quilt. Press toward the border. Sew the top and bottom borders to the quilt. Press toward the border.

Finish the Quilt

1. Mark quilting designs on the quilt top or plan to stitch without marking.

2. Make the quilt backing.

3. Create a quilt sandwich by layering the pieced top, batting, and backing. Secure the sandwich together using your preferred method of basting to prevent shifting while you are quilting.

4. Quilt by hand or machine.

> **TIP**
>
> *If you chose to use trapunto when appliquéing your motifs, do not cross over the edges of your motif when quilting. This will reduce the impact of the trapunto.*

BINDING

Square up the quilt. Make and apply the binding; finish by hand or machine.

Carolyn finished her quilt with a hand-stitched contrast color binding. It frames the quilt so it pops like paintings stuck on the fridge, or like an art gallery.

While this quilt was made for Jacob, it's awfully hard to pass on something that is a true reflection of time spent together creating. That moment, that brushstroke, that hand on the fabric … the process is definitely as important as the outcome in this case.

CAROLYN … ON IMPROV

I like improvisational piecing because I like the idea of maybe not knowing all the exact steps ahead of time. Instead, I like the idea of having a starting point and moving forward with an openness to where it might take you along the way.

CAROLYN … ON CHALLENGES

I do think it's important to set something aside if it's not clicking or working out. Usually I find that space can bring clarity when that happens.

The truth is that I really like being in the right mental space for a project before I begin. I find it really satisfying when an idea has had some time to simmer, whether that's hours, days, or years—yes, some ideas take that long to find their way into play!

QUILTMAKER
Carolyn Friedlander

Photo by Carolyn Friedlander

Carolyn is an architect turned pattern designer turned fabric designer with an eye for detail and a style that turns heads in the quilt industry. She turned to quilting in 2009, following school and work in St. Louis. In short order she launched her company producing patterns and stamps. She has since further branched out as a licensed fabric designer, lecturer, and teacher.

Residing in her home state of Florida, she lives in an old farm house, adding her own style to the place. This keeps her close to her family, including her nephew Jacob—who is always ready to play with fabric with his aunt, allowing them to collaborate on the project for this book.

Visit Carolyn's website at carolynfriedlander.com.

CAROLYN...ON INSPIRATION

There are people who influence my quilting, but what I think influences it the most is curiosity. Curiosity about how something will work out, how to put something together, or how to express something that is in my head is what is behind everything I make. Curiosity is what pushes me to the sewing machine or keeps a needle in my hand, because I become so devoted to solving whatever problem is brewing in my mind.

A STORY WITH NO END

INSPIRATION

"We already had a quilt on our king-size bed, but when you put two adults under it and add in some middle-of-the-night munchkins, it quickly became a battle for the covers. Someone was always left with a cold backside. Not to mention that the lack of overhang made it hard to make the bed look good. It should be noted that the person most accused of hogging the covers was not my husband or my children.

The not-quite-big-enough bed quilt was made from blocks sent in for our 2002 wedding. I used our anniversary as the inspiration for making a new, *larger* quilt with plenty of overhang and a lot of meaning. We all know that X's and O's represent "hugs and kisses" when signing a letter, so I used that idea, plus colors pulled from our own history. Being able to make a quilt with this much personal meaning, and then seeing it in everyday use, is powerful. I actually smile when making the bed, and not because I like that much neatness. I think about the stories that have gotten us to this point—back to our wedding and then some—and I imagine the stories the quilt will share as we go.

PROCESS

Thankfully, our wedding wasn't in a lost vortex of style or color trends. There was, and is, nothing pastel about us. So to surprise my husband with this anniversary present, I referred back to our wedding colors: red, orange, and hot pink.

This quilt started with the idea of the X block for a kiss and an understanding that it would be a king-size quilt. That's it. Otherwise it was a just a stack of fabric next to a rotary cutter.

NOTE

This concept is easily sized down if a king-size quilt is not what you need. Simply start with a background piece of fabric about 4˝–6˝ larger than what you want your finished blocks to be and still be flexible with the desired finished size. The insertion of the X's can change the size of the blocks significantly.

CHERYL...ON TOOLS

I rarely use a seam ripper, not because I'm flawless—far from it—but because I would rather save time by simply cutting away my accident. This works great when improvising. If I'm precision piecing, I'll set aside the accident and make another. Always go forward, not backward.

Photos by Cheryl Arkison

CHERYL ARKISON

KISSES

FINISHED BLOCK: 35˝ × 30˝

FINISHED QUILT: 105˝ × 90˝

Materials Required

- **Prints in red, orange, and hot pink:** 1 yard each of 9 fabrics for backgrounds

- **Light fabrics:** 2 yards total for kisses

- **Backing fabric:** 8¼ yards

- **Binding fabric:** 1 yard

- **Batting:** 109˝ × 94˝

Cutting Instructions

WOF = width of fabric

PRINTS:

- Cut off the selvages from each 1-yard piece.

LIGHT FABRICS:

- Cut 18 strips 3˝–5˝ wide × WOF. (There is no need to measure the strips, but do use a ruler to cut them straight.)

BINDING:

- Cut 11 strips 2½˝ × WOF.

CHERYL…ON FAMILY

Morgan and I have been together the entire time I've been a quilter. What started as a hobby is now a career. It was one thing when I sewed a couple of quilts a year, and quite another when we have to have picnics on the living room floor because I can't quite clean up the projects on the dining room table.

With a separate space now, the mess of creativity is somewhat contained but my husband and kids also have space to gather for all the quilting action. At first I thought this space would be my domain alone, but like sharing my sketchbook with the kids, sharing my studio has become a more realistic adventure. And one that captures the family perfectly.

ASSEMBLY

Make the Blocks

1. Press a 1-yard piece of background fabric. Place it on a cutting mat with the selvage edges on the sides and the cut edges on the top and bottom. Using a rotary cutter and ruler, slice through the middle of the fabric at an angle somewhere between 85° and 60°. Do not cut it straight through the middle, vertically, as your goal is to create an X in the final block (not an L or T). Sew a light strip to a cut edge.

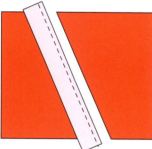

Add first strip.

> **TIP**
>
> *The more of an angle you cut, the more you will have to trim from your block when squaring up.*

2. Sew the other side of the light strip to the other cut edge. Press toward the light strip.

3. Cut through the middle of the pieced fabric at an opposing angle. Sew another light strip to those cut edges. Press toward the light strip.

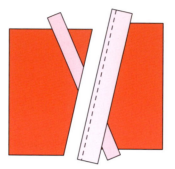

Add second strip.

4. When you sew the second seam of this strip, match up the seams of the first kisses strip as best you can. Do not match up the edges of the background fabric. Sew both edges and press toward the light strip.

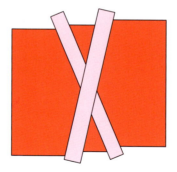

Matching first strip seams

5. Repeat using the 8 other 1-yard pieces of background fabric to make 9 blocks total.

Assemble the Quilt Top

1. Square up the blocks to measure 35½˝ × 30½˝. Since your blocks may be different, measure them all first to make sure you can trim to a consistent size. If the blocks are larger than your ruler, try making a template from paper, lightweight cardboard, or freezer paper. It is easier to make the paper rectangle first and then use it to square up your quilt block.

> ### TIP
>
> *Depending on the angles of your kisses, you may have to cut off big chunks of fabric from the blocks to get the edges straight. That's okay! Keep these for the quilt back or add them to the scrap bin.*

2. Arrange and sew the blocks into 3 rows of 3 blocks each. Press. Join the rows. Press.

BINDING

Square up the quilt. Make and apply the binding; finish by hand or machine.

I actually struggled for a while when picking the binding for this quilt because of the vibrant colors. In the end, however, I went for high contrast in a seemingly unrelated color. I did the same thing with the backing fabric. It tones down the heat of the front and adds a somewhat masculine touch to the quilt.

Finish the Quilt

1. Make the quilt backing.

2. Make a quilt sandwich by layering the pieced top, batting, and backing. Secure the sandwich together using your preferred method of basting to prevent shifting while you are quilting.

3. This is a large quilt, so you may want to consider taking it to a longarm quilter. However, it can be quilted on a domestic machine by breaking the quilting down into sections and embracing the time it will take. I used pebble designs throughout the quilting to add the hugs (O's) to go with the kisses.

CHERYL…ON MAKING MISTAKES

The best way to avoid mistakes—although they really are inevitable for all of us—is to know when to sew. I'm a morning person, for example, so late-night sewing is generally a recipe for disaster. But if that's the only time I've got, I save the mindless work for then and plan or cut fabric when my brain is fresher.

You Inspire Me to Quilt

ABOUT THE AUTHOR

Although happily considered a modern quilter, Cheryl produces work that spans several techniques. She is in love with scraps, circles, and improvisational piecing. The ability to just sit and sew is what gets her through the day, even when that sewing comes without a plan or any reason. It always comes together (eventually).

Cheryl is a quilter and writer. She writes and teaches on quilting, craft, creativity, food, and family. And it all comes from her dining room empire in her crowded, colorful house. From this space she wrote her first book, *Sunday Morning Quilts* (co-authored with Amanda Jean Nyberg) and her second book, *A Month of Sundays*. She also regularly contributes articles and patterns to numerous magazines.

At home, she is mother to two wild little girls and an adventurous boy. Her husband puts up with her quilting because he gets cold in the evenings. Visit her website at cherylarkison.com.

ABOUT THE PHOTOGRAPHER

Kate Inglis got halfway through the photography diploma program at Vancouver's Langara College before moving back east and writing books. She found her way back to the camera as a founding contributor to Shutter Sisters and co-authored *Expressive Photography: The Shutter Sisters Guide to Shooting from the Heart*. Her first published solo photography credit is her work featured throughout Cheryl Arkison's book *A Month of Sundays*.

For several years, Kate has photographed families, portraits, and weddings (when not writing about pirates and monsters). She has led photography workshops at Pen & Paper in Manzanita, Oregon; at Serendipity and Squam by the Sea retreats along the Outer Banks of North Carolina; for the Halifax-based Atlantic Photographic Education Group; and at her own seaside shed in Nova Scotia. Visit her website at kateinglis.com.

Other books by Cheryl:

 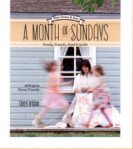

stashBOOKS®

fabric arts for a handmade lifestyle

If you're craving beautiful authenticity in a time of mass-production...Stash Books is for you. Stash Books is a line of how-to books celebrating fabric arts for a handmade lifestyle. Backed by C&T Publishing's solid reputation for quality, Stash Books will inspire you with contemporary designs, clear and simple instructions, and engaging photography.

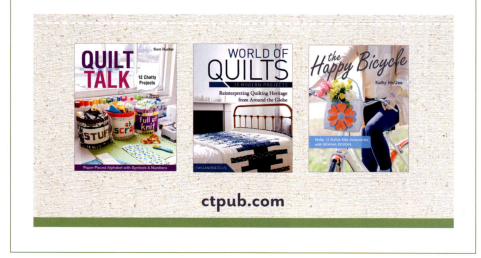

ctpub.com